Frank sinatra

a celebration

Project Editor: Tessa Rose
Copy Editor: Nigel Matheson
Project Art Direction: Russell Porter
Design: Fiona Knowles
Picture Research: Sharon Hutton
Production: Garry Lewis

Printed and bound in Italy

Carlton Books Limited
20 St Anne's Court
Wardour Street

Acknowledgements

In such a venture as SINATRA: A CELEBRATION, the author's own endeavours can
be rendered next-to-useless without the invaluable assistance of any number of
helpers. The following list comprises a group of people whose eagerness to assist
with all manner of inquiries – often made at the most inconvenient times – was
matched only by their desire to produce accuracy, full detail and as speedy a
delivery as possible. If my sometimes fading memory has omitted deserving names,
I can only trust that they will not be offended and they themselves will know that
their noble efforts will have contributed to the book's overall compilation and
factual accuracy.

Dale Belcher, Doreen Browne, Sammy Cahn, Don Costa, Fred Dellar, Robert
Farnon, Alan A Freeman, Dave Gelly, Dorothy Gosling, Chris Howes, Billy May,
Loonis McGlohon, Rod McKuen, Henry Pleasants, Nelson Riddle, J Billy Verplanck;
George Adey, Ken Barnes, Colin Britt, Robin Britt, Trisha Coogan (Sony/UK), Allan
Garrick; Jo Kennedy (BMG/UK), Brian O'Connor, Jo Pratt (EMI Records/UK), Ray
Purslow (Record Centre, Birmingham), Tony Radcliffe.

I WOULD also be lacking in common courtesy should I fail to express my deep
gratitude to my new-found friends at Carlton Books, London. To Sharon Hutton,
for assembling the range of marvellous photos to be found throughout the book.
To Fiona Knowles, for a superbly creative layout-and-design job. To copy editor
Nigel Matheson and, in particular, to my long-suffering project editor, Tessa Rose,
for constant guidance, editing expertise and, above all, infinite patience as the
book grew. In every way, they've been a Top Team!

To: MEB

*Without whose inspiration, especially during what will
remain my own Golden Years, this book - like life itself -
would have been absolutely impossible ...*

CARLTON

stan britt

contents

Overture

What this book actually celebrates is the undeniable fact that, for close on six decades, one of the all-time great singing talents has continued to be such a compelling factor in the lives of so many people.

As Sinatra approaches 80, this book endeavours to put into perspective just what an awesome contribution this native North-American-of-Sicilian-extraction has made to the world of entertainment.

And if the emphasis here falls principally on Sinatra's personal achievements in raising pop vocalism to an art form, then that's nothing to apologise for. Few if any artists have been as productive over as many years. The one regret is that these pages can cover only a tiny number of the 1001 events that have made up such a lengthy and industrious career.

Sinatra: A Celebration traces the boyhood days in Hoboken, New Jersey, through the myriad of often complex, occasionally tortuous and always intriguing stories that culminated in Sinatra being crowned the King of Show Business.

But this book doesn't claim to be a blow-by-blow account of Sinatra's action-packed personal life. Far too much literature has been published in previous years relating to Sinatra's private affairs. Whether true or false, much too much of it has been sensational, revealing little about the man's professional talents, let alone what really makes him run.

And, throughout all the highs and lows, one thing is certain: Sinatra has proved himself the supreme individualist, willing to take risks. All the while, he's done it *his* way…

Of course, there have been times when Sinatra has been less than gracious to many people… frequently towards the press, sometimes even to friends. A hugely-inflated ego complemented by a temper of legendary violence has often combined with circumstance to get him into deep trouble. He has had his fair share of fights – both verbal and physical – and sometimes in public. A reckless attitude has occasionally resulted in disaster.

In Sinatra's defence, he has on occasion openly confessed to his failings. And conversely, he has always given generously to charity.

In any case, even if many of the "bad" stories about Sinatra are true, they are of minimal interest to this author. Let others write those…

Occasional references *are* made here to Sinatra's alleged involvement with the underworld, or his attempts to seek gaming licences in the lucrative pastures of Las Vegas. But even these somehow correlate to what this book is all about: the man and his music.

As one of the greatest ever vocalists, Sinatra's contributions may never be surpassed. As a genuinely gifted actor, he made a substantial contribution to Hollywood – winning one Oscar and receiving another Academy Award nomination. But his acting skills have only rarely approached his genius as a singer, especially in concert and as a recording artist.

Light and shade – Sinatra's has been a life of celebrity and of achievement.

This book, then, is for those who have been touched, deeply or just casually, by his talents – primarily by his unique qualities as a singer. For above all, he remains the Poet Laureate of the Popular Song.

Sinatra
the Voice
of Popular
Music

Sinatra, c. 1944. The personalized chair at MGM defines his greatest single talent.

Even before he came into his own as a performer, Frank Sinatra always sounded like Frank Sinatra and nobody else.

Originally, though, it was Bing Crosby who triggered off Sinatra's unstoppable quest to become the very best singer around. Following a trip to Jersey City to see the incomparable crooner in concert, Sinatra discovered his destiny.

Impressed by Crosby's persuasive way with a song, Sinatra vowed that his own approach to singing would be equally individualistic. He would be beholden to no other performer for his style, not even the all-powerful, much-imitated Crosby.

It is worth remembering that until the emergence of Sinatra at the end of the Thirties, Crosby had been the reigning King of Pop Vocalism and, together with Louis Armstrong, Billie Holiday and Al Jolson, one of the great innovators of his craft.

Bing could swing with the best of them but his real magic was reserved for ballads. As his voice deepened with the years, developing real warmth and tonal quality, he became the first pop-vocal superstar of the Thirties and reigned as undisputed King until Sinatra's arrival on the scene ...

But, although Crosby's ability to project songs made a profound impression, this was not the way Frank Sinatra wanted to sing. Even at an early stage, Sinatra had strong views about not becoming just another Crosby clone – he would attempt a completely different approach.

As he told *Life International* magazine, some 30 years after that milestone Crosby concert, "I decided to experiment a little and come up with something different. What I finally hit upon was more the *bel canto* Italian school of singing, without making a point of it. That meant I had to stay in better shape because I had to sing more. It was more difficult than Crosby's style, much more difficult."

The style he came up with has indeed been compared to the Italian *bel canto* ("beautiful singing") form of operatic singing, characterized by its rich tonal lyricism and a bravura display of vocal technique.

Henry Pleasants, the noted vocal-music expert, detects *bel canto* influence in Sinatra's work. In a personal interview with the author during the late-Seventies, he cited Sinatra's "absolute mastery of the use of *appoggiatura* – when a singer inserts an extra note between two other notes – thus giving expressive emphasis, and elegance, to a cadence. Just as important, he was always aware of when best to use it ... and when not to."

Crosby provided the trigger for Sinatra's career in showbusiness. Without doubt, Sinatra's seamless phrasing was, as Pleasants insists, uncannily close to the Italian vocal school. However, there were two important ingredients of Sinatra's style which were not considered obligatory in *bel canto*. Firstly, his insistence on setting emotion above mere technique; and, secondly, his joyous brand of musical humour – something for which *bel canto* singing is hardly renowned.

In fact, Sinatra went to great lengths to build up his "effortless" brand of singing. In the same *Life International* interview, he recalled how deeply affected he was by the *legato* ballad-playing of his former boss, orchestra leader Tommy Dorsey. "He would take a musical phrase and play it all the way through seemingly without breathing, for 8, 10 or maybe 16 bars."

Mabel Mercer – her impeccable diction had a profound influence on Sinatra's style.

Close scrutiny during the two-and-a-half years he spent with the famous trombonist's band – constantly trying to figure out how Dorsey breathed through a held note – convinced Sinatra that this was the kind of phrasing he needed for his own singing style. To achieve extra lung-power, he swam regularly, including much time spent holding his breath under water, and worked out frequently at a local running track.

From the outset, Frank Sinatra's approach to singing was supremely conversational. Without neglecting the melodic line or the need to imbue a performance with rhythm and swing, the words were of top concern at all times.

To this end, Sinatra perfected his own special kind of diction. Consonants, rather than vowels, were always stressed. But however individual his singing became, his influences should not be forgotten. Crosby of course provided the springboard for his aspirations but it was from Mabel Mercer that Sinatra learned about diction. Through years of performing in small, intimate New York clubs, Mabel Mercer had established a near-legendary reputation for putting across lyrics with conviction.

Pianist-composer Loonis McGlohan has made a living out of providing sensitive, eloquent accompaniments for top-class singers.

"I learned about leaving breathing space for singers by listening to singers breathe. Particularly Mabel Mercer. You've got to wait to hear where they breathe. Sometimes they'd put a comma in a different place ... Mabel and Frank – I have to lock them together in this instance – would always do the proper punctuation in a song. And I'm sure Frank learned a lot about this from Mabel."

However much he learned from Mercer and Crosby, Sinatra's biggest debt was owed to Billie Holiday. He was deeply affected by her innate sense of timing and the heart-on-sleeve approach she took to singing, especially the kind of sad ballads which he would make his own as the years unfolded. Billie sang about life in the raw, with a couldn't-give-a-damn style that must have appealed to Frank's own brand of arrogance.

Sinatra found Holiday a kindred spirit in other basic ways. For, as his own talent began to unfold, the sexual content in his delivery grew stronger and more obvious to rivals hers. Like Billie Holiday too, Sinatra has all too often operated on a short fuse. This, together with his own Sicilian background, no doubt gave his singing added bite and, from the Fifties on, a visceral edge that communicated itself to audiences.

Sinatra has openly acknowledged his debt to Lady Day. During an interview with *Ebony* magazine in 1958, he declared,

> *"With few exceptions, every major pop singer in the United States during her generation has been touched in some way by her genius. It is Billie Holiday, whom I first heard in 52nd Street clubs in the early-Thirties, who was, and still remains, the greatest single musical influence on me."*

Early on, as a singer with Harry James and Tommy Dorsey, Sinatra's ambitions were held in check by a fairly rigid stylistic format that allowed little scope for self-expression. Numbers were confined for the most part to what dance band musicians once called jig tempo – a basic medium-paced, restrained swing.

"All Or Nothing At All" remains the best-known of the nine items Sinatra recorded with James. And even though he had not yet developed into a true lyric-interpreter, there was no doubting the unrestrained passion of his delivery, or the obvious sincerity in his reading of the words.

With both James and Dorsey, Sinatra's speciality was always as a ballad singer. From a rhythmic standpoint, he showed little outstanding ability initially, although he handled himself adequately in this area.

Sinatra may have been an incomplete swinger at this stage but his singing on songs like "East Of The Sun" (arranged by Sy Oliver) and "Head On My Pillow" (with a chart by Axel Stordahl) does not embarrass him. Wisely, he chose to relax and allow the fine rhythmic impulses radiated by drummer Buddy Rich, pianist Joe Bushkin and the rest of the rhythm section to do the rest.

By the mid-Forties, Sinatra was well on his way to fusing all the elements into a totally individual vocal style. It remains something of an unexplained mystery to this writer that there are certain long-time Sinatra admirers who tend to gloss over his singing during the Forties. In terms of pure vocal quality, his work from this time has rarely been surpassed.

True, the voice sometimes lacked the full-bodied quality that was to come: the extra depth of expression and know-how that would illuminate his singing from the Fifties onwards was not readily apparent in the Forties. And an ability to produce satisfying rhythm performances was something of a rarity. But when it came to ballads, with his right-hand man, arranger Axel Stordahl, in almost uncanny rapport, Sinatra could do little wrong.

One of the encouraging aspects of his recordings during this halcyon period was that he not only recorded the new pops of the day (including those emanating from Broadway and Hollywood), but he also breathed new life into oldies such as "Embraceable You", "Someone To Watch Over Me", "You Go To My

Happy reunion. Sinatra swings again with Harry James – live, in Los Angeles, 1979.

Head", "These Foolish Things" and "She's Funny That Way". And the boundless confidence of the man enabled him to embrace more ambitious works such as "Bess, Oh Where's My Bess?" (from *Porgy & Bess*), "Ol' Man River" (*Showboat*) and the extended "Soliloquy" from *Carousel*.

Whatever you think of Sinatra, one thing is absolutely certain: he remains the single greatest live performer, past, present and, one can safely venture, for the foreseeable future. The greatest live performer, let us be clear, not greatest live entertainer.

Not that Sinatra doesn't entertain – far from it. But he doesn't play piano or a guitar or any kind of musical instrument. Nor does he dance, juggle, or perform magical tricks. He has had a fairly snappy line in comedy at his concerts for decades but this was a regular part of his concert programme, principally to allow him to catch his breath along the way and to introduce his accompanists.

No, Frank Sinatra just sings. And, therefore, he has been able to totally commit his talents to doing just that one thing.

Scarcely a dynamic personality in his early days, it's perhaps odd that at that time Sinatra had such an extraordinary ability to communicate with his audiences. It was more than just his singing voice. To many, he may have been an unimposing figure – a skinny young man, whose on-stage persona was that of a somewhat fragile, unassertive guy clinging to a stand-up mike ... who just sang.

Yet it was that quality of vulnerability which created immediate rapport with his audience during the band-singing years – an audience which was comprised mostly, though not exclusively, of young women. Part of that appeal could be explained by his country's involvement in World War II and the relative absence of young men. But there was more to the Sinatra phenomenon.

In some media quarters, it used to be obligatory to review Sinatra's appearances in terms of his lack of *avoirdupois*, to criticize the way he dressed and, of course, the near-hysterical reactions of his bobbysox-clad fans. Only the more discerning newspaper critics and the quality jazz magazines talked about his vocal technique, or his distinctive approach on-stage.

Taking it easy – Sinatra relaxes backstage before a gig, and in the recording studio.

Even after he'd decided on a solo career, the critics clung to their view of this shy little guy and the silly little teenagers, who'd one day grow up and forget about their Frankie. Those kind of critics would have been shocked by the suggestion that part of Sinatra's appeal lay in the sexual content of his work.

After his Oscar-winning role in *From Here To Eternity* came a remarkable professional metamorphosis – he began to be taken seriously. Although the brash, hard-drinking, arrogant personality that now emerged was, we are told, already well-known to friends and colleagues, the kind of visceral, hard-swinging singer that emerged as the "new" Sinatra produced a *volte-face* among critics, who had so often put the boot in before.

Suddenly, Sinatra was The Man. And, critics queued up to have their names put on the door at venues where he was appearing. It is common knowledge that Sinatra himself was hip to this sudden reappraisal: he never forgave those who'd put him down – especially during the dark days.

But Sinatra rarely disappointed those who came to his gigs. On-stage, his deportment was impeccable. Even just the way he'd walk from one side of a stage to the other was an event. His occasional use of a small handful of props – like the combination of a stool, a lighted cigarette and a glass of some undetermined liquid – enabled him with great subtlety and effectiveness to create a bar-room scene, or enhance what were invariably definitive readings of classic saloon songs like "Angel Eyes" or "One For My Baby".

One of Sinatra's most significant on-stage gifts was his unparalleled use of the hand-microphone. During his earliest days, Sinatra had realized the potential for relaying even the most *sotto voce* phrase by sophisticated use of the microphone. In those days, vocalists perforce used microphones of the strictly stand-up variety – usually square-shaped and attached to a length of piping and a base.

During his *Life International* interview in 1965, Sinatra emphasized how "tremendously important" the use of a microphone was. Many singers, he said, never learned. "They never understood, and still don't, that a microphone is their instrument. It's like they are part of an orchestra, but instead of playing a saxophone they're playing a microphone."

And his perfectionist approach to this aspect of live performance stretched to using a black microphone, "so that it will melt into my dinner jacket and the audience isn't aware of it ... " Sinatra's interest in what could be done with this "instrument" had begun on the fateful occasion when he first went to see Crosby in concert: we don't know how Crosby used his microphone in Jersey

City, but it was impressive enough to exercise a profound influence over Frank's career.

Sinatra, out of retirement in the Seventies, sings again, in Paris.

Even in his "shy guy" days, Frank Sinatra always exuded a kind of charisma. But from the Fifties and thereafter his charisma became a significant element in concert. Whether on-stage at the Sands or Caesar's Palace – his two most frequent ports of call on the Las Vegas circuit – or at Carnegie Hall or the Royal Festival Hall, wherever he went, he generated the kind of electricity which few others can match. Even before he made his entry, the air was often charged with excitement. And if he was feeling good, the voice was in tip-top shape and the audience was responsive, there would be a quality that is best described as "magic".

Little wonder, then, that it's so often been said that there was no other place on earth where Frank Sinatra found more happiness and fulfilment than performing on stage before a large audience, and with a large orchestra behind him.

Sinatra's own philosophy about performing was summarised in a comment he made years ago: "If you want to get an audience with you, there's only one way. You have to reach out to them with total honesty and humility. You can be the most artistically perfect performer in the world, but an audience is like a broad – if you're indifferent, endsville!"

Rarely have musicians who have worked alongside Sinatra had anything but praise for the way he goes about his job. Indeed, long ago he set the standard for live performance by not only insisting on his own key musicians, but also by naming and fully crediting the composers and arrangers of each song on-stage. And though he might be critical of mistakes by others, he has always been generous with his praise.

Talk with singers, musicians, songwriters or arrangers and you'll find that each one has a particular reason for admiring Sinatra's singing. Although most musical persons enjoy his rhythmic work, by far the largest majority state a marked preference for his way with a ballad. In this context, it's his matchless skills at musical storytelling which come out on top.

But it was *Songs For Young Lovers*, Sinatra's first micro-groove LP and his first album for Capitol, that showed he was eminently capable of producing superb, loosely-swinging work to put him on a par with practically any of his contemporaries.

Songs For Swingin' Lovers was not only his most popular album from any period but it enabled Sinatra to prove his rhythmic point in the company of his most famous musical associate Nelson Riddle. The combination produced some of the most glorious recorded vocal-instrumental music ever produced.

By the time he laid down those tracks, Sinatra had come up with a highly-personal, dynamic method of swinging. It wasn't totally jazz – but it certainly swung! Indeed, there were occasions when he produced swing-singing as good as the best out-and-out jazz vocalists – occasionally, even better.

Writer-broadcaster Dave Gelly once described Sinatra's approach to swing for the author as being "a very businesslike thing". At the same time, he compared it to the no-nonsense, straight-ahead jazz players like Harry Edison, Ben Webster and Zoot Sims. "It's that sort of unfussy singing – there's very little in the way of decoration. It's all down to a precise placement of notes in relation to rhythm, so that you get a song to swing.

"The magical way that Sinatra does this involves both the precise placement of notes and an ability to reflect the conversational nature of the song. This is his thing, and something which he shares with a very short list of other singers, a highly-distinguished group of whom the supreme example is Billie ... When you see him in person, and he's singing songs which swing, the sort of note-placement that Miles Davis had, is what he's got."

Ultimately, though, in any serious reassessment of Sinatra, it

comes down to the ballads to provide the final definition of his art. From the Fifties, one can cite, not just individual tracks, but whole LPs: *In The Wee Small Hours*; *Close To You*; *Where Are You?*; *No One Cares*; *Point Of No Return*.

In subsequent years, Sinatra's recordings – like his concert repertoire – have provided fascinating examples of his musical flexibility. Not all of them have proved a complete success. But Sinatra never was afraid to make the occasional error of judgement – indeed at times he seems to have positively courted disaster.

At least, though, he didn't lack the guts to try something new. Now, in his 80th year, it appears we shall not be seeing – or hearing – from Frank Sinatra again as a concert artist. Sad though that prospect is, it has been obvious for some time that not even Sinatra can keep on putting the clock back.

It is all too easy to trot out the cliché-of-clichés: we shall never see or hear another Frank Sinatra in our lifetimes. But it is true. Certainly, we now have to judge him as a vocalist of unmatched achievements, someone who long since elevated himself into the area of total respect reserved for the great classical or opera performers of this century.

It is true also because the set of circumstances, which came together long ago in a New Jersey port, will never occur again. For better or worse, the action-packed life and times of Francis Albert Sinatra can never be repeated.

Perhaps the best summation was made many years ago, by another truly great singer of the 20th-century and the person who triggered off his burning zeal to become the greatest in his field, Bing Crosby.

"Frank Sinatra is the kind of singer who comes along once in a lifetime – but why did it have to be my lifetime?"

The
Embryonic
Sinatra

Francis Albert Sinatra was born in Hoboken, New Jersey, on December 12, 1915, the only child of immigrants Martin and Nathalie ("Dolly") Sinatra.

Young Francis Albert poses with Mama – and not a smile in sight.

One way or another, Frank Sinatra has achieved a lasting reputation as a fighter. This started the day he was born, weighing in at an impressive 13-and-a-half pounds. Being so large, his birth was difficult and forceps had to be used for the delivery, resulting in permanent scarring on the left side of Sinatra's head.

Much more alarming, though, was the fact that Baby Sinatra hadn't uttered a sound; nor indeed did he appear to be breathing. With enviable presence of mind, Rosa Garavente, Dolly Sinatra's mother, lifted an apparently lifeless infant body, then ran cold water over it. At once, the Sinatra vocal cords sprang into action for the first time.

Hoboken was a tough place to grow up. With its labyrinth of railway marshalling yards and factory buildings, it was a dreary, grimy port, not far from Jersey City but separated from the bright lights of New York City and Manhattan by the wide Hudson River. For most of his working life, Martin Sinatra was employed at the Hoboken Fire Department. In his spare time, he was also a prize-fighter – under the name of "Marty O'Brien". Dolly Sinatra exercised strict control over young Frank, who tended to be something of a loner. From an early age, he learnt to stand up for himself.

By all accounts, Sinatra was a modest pupil, first, at the David E Rue Junior High School, from which he graduated in January, 1931. Later the same year, he dropped out of the A J Demarest High School (in his sophomore year). And, apart from a short period spent at the Drake Business School, that was where his formal education ended.

Career-wise, Sinatra wasn't sure what to do. He was briefly employed on the staff of the local *Jersey Observer* as a truck loader and copy-boy. He also worked as an apprentice ship's riveter. In fact, the youthful Sinatra's mind was on other things. He loved the cinema and music had begun to exert an ever-increasing influence on his thinking. The acquisition of a ukulele, given him by an uncle at 15, provided the incentive to try his hand at singing. Sinatra used to accompany himself as he attempted to reproduce the songs he was hearing day by day on the wireless –

from the likes of Gene Austin, Rudy Vallee, Russ Columbo and, above all, Bing Crosby.

Francis A. Sinatra with Demarest High's glee club.

Indeed, it was after Sinatra had taken regular girlfriend Nancy Barbato to see Crosby live at Loew's Theater in Jersey City in March 1934, that the die was finally cast. Watching Crosby perform, Sinatra became convinced that he too had the kind of talent to make it to the top.

However, it took six years of hard work before Frank Sinatra gained his first real toe-hold on the ladder to success.

To get started, Sinatra had to take his courage in both hands and present himself on-stage at numerous amateur or semi-pro talent contests. These took place in a variety of venues, often in noisy roadhouses and social clubs, and most of the time Sinatra was performing for nothing more than a bite to eat.

During these formative years, Sinatra single-mindedly sought out as much exposure as possible. He even did *unpaid* live appearances, anything that would bring his name and voice before a wider audience.

A major stepping-stone was his appearance on a popular, long-running radio show called *Major Bowes And His Original Amateur Hour*. Broadcast by NBC, the show was an open invitation to possible fame and fortune for hundreds of aspiring performers.

Sinatra auditioned for the contest at New York's Capitol Theater and passed with ease. Major Bowes suggested he join

forces with a vocal trio from Hoboken, known as the Three Flashes. Soon the Three Flashes died and the Hoboken Four were born in their stead.

"Frank Sinatra Day", 10 October 1947: Fire Captain Martin Sinatra crowns his son's day.

The new group – with Frank singing lead – appeared at the next *Amateur Hour* event on September 8, 1935. They sang the Mack/Brown/Dabney original, "Shine", immortalized by Louis Armstrong, and won the contest hands down. Their victory was the biggest in the history of the competition and the Hoboken Four joined Bowes' regular travelling troupe.

Sinatra's membership of the Hoboken Four only lasted for a couple of months, the time it took the group to reach the West Coast. By then, the lead vocalist was bored with the routine of touring. One report has suggested matters came to a head after a heated dispute between Sinatra and the others: they were beginning to resent his growing popularity - he was just getting to like it.

In the end, Sinatra left abruptly for home. Reunited with family and friends, he was ready to make a second attempt at a career in singing – this time as a *solo* singer!

Despite disapproving of her son's ambitions, Dolly Sinatra gave Frank $65 to purchase his own portable public-address system. Always forward-thinking, Sinatra added his own personal library of printed orchestrations ("stocks") for use by any of the accompanying bands with which he found employment.

For a while, Sinatra held down a regular job at the Union, a Hoboken social club, earning $40 a week. This ended after Sinatra failed to persuade the management to install facilities that would allow him to broadcast from the premises. He had more success persuading the bosses of several stations in the New York and New Jersey areas to allow him to perform on radio ... for nothing.

His next two moves were of real significance. First, he landed a regular job at the Rustic Cabin, a popular roadhouse, not too far from Alpine, New Jersey. Even at the audition, he was quick to note that the Rustic Cabin had facilities for broadcasting. Then, on February 4, 1939, Sinatra wed Nancy Barbato at Our Lady of Sorrows Catholic Church, Jersey City.

At the Cabin, Sinatra was kept busy for his $15-a-week-plus-tips. He sang solo, of course, with the resident Harold Arden Orchestra. But he also acted as master of ceremonies and showed customers to their tables.

Towards the end of the 18-month residency, one of Sinatra's local broadcasts paid off handsomely. His singing was heard on the radio one evening by a tall, whippet-thin trumpet player/band leader, who was listening in on his hotel radio. After establishing an international reputation with Benny Goodman, Harry James had recently put together his own big-band.

At this time, James badly needed a good, reliable boy singer, and so he decided on a visit to the Rustic Cabin, together with his manager. Both were highly impressed. Right away, they asked Sinatra if he would join the Harry James Orchestra. Salary: $75 a week. Almost immediately, a two-year contract was drawn up and signed ... and the roadhouse lost its personable, super-confident young singer. Sinatra raced home to break the news to Nancy at their three-room apartment home in Jersey City. Now, he told her, the days of hustling radio stations were over. And there would be no more waiter jobs.

The gig with James was just the kind of break Frank had been working his butt off to get. And, no doubt, he told Nancy,

"This is just the first step, honey. Now, I'm on my way..."

RETROSPECTIVES
1935-1939

GIGS

Very little material has surfaced which gives more than an inkling of the kind of singing voice Sinatra possessed before he joined the Harry James Orchestra. Indeed, there are just two examples of his work with the Hoboken Four. Both emanate from appearances on the *Amateur Hour* shows.

The first – and best-known – is "Shine", recorded at New York's Capital Theater on September 8, 1935. After Sinatra had self-consciously introduced the group, the Hoboken Four produced an up-tempo, somewhat dated version of the jazz-based standard. The performance gives little indication of greater things to come. The same can be said of the treatment they meted out to "The Curse Of An Aching Heart", broadcast some time later in 1935.

Both numbers, however, are now of enormous historical interest

and available on albums such as the British-made CD, *1935-1939: The Beginnings And Harry James*.

More revealing, perhaps – and contained within the same CD release – is "Our Love", co-written by Larry Clinton, Buddy Bernier and Bob Emmerich and freely adapted from Tchaikovsky's *Romeo And Juliet*. This was recorded privately by Sinatra as a demo disc with orchestral accompaniment by Frank Manne. There *are* elements of the Sinatra-to-come on this rare disc – which, presumably, he (or Dolly) must have paid for. The production of demo discs by up-and-coming performers was something of a rarity in 1939 – even private demos.

It was a further indication of just how dedicated the young man from Hoboken, NJ, was to getting on in show business ...

MOVIES

Sinatra's earliest involvement with motion pictures came from his association with Major Bowes. He took part in two shorts, under the collective heading of *Major Bowes' Amateur Theatre Off The Air* (both made in 1935 and released through RKO). Young Sinatra played a waiter in the first and then "blacked-up" for a bit part in *The Big Minstrel Act*.

RECORDINGS

Of all the rare early performances, which have turned up in recent times, the most bizarre is included on a CD, aptly titled *The Rarest Sinatra*. Taken from a *Town Hall Tonight* show, it features Sinatra conducting the Four Sharps, a less-than-promising Dixieland-jazz outfit. Under Sinatra's supervision, the Sharps go through an awful version of "Exactly Like You".

For more than one obvious reason, this song is just about the rarest of all the rare Sinatra "performances" ... !

The Band-Singing Years

ON NUMEROUS occasions over the years, Frank Sinatra has been delighted to reaffirm that the six months he spent with the Harry James Orchestra were among the happiest of all his musical experiences.

For one thing, Sinatra found Harry James to be a friendly and supportive leader. James, a native of Albany, Georgia, knew he'd signed a most promising vocalist and wanted to encourage him as much as possible. There was one sticky moment when James suggested it might, perhaps, be helpful if the singer changed his name. Sinatra was appalled – and adamant. It was the name he'd been born with and it was the name he would continue to use forever – in *every* area of his life. His new boss soon got the message ...

Harry Haag James (1916-83) had established an enviable reputation as a superbly-gifted, fiery trumpet soloist with the star-studded Benny Goodman Orchestra. His early background found him helping his father, a bandmaster, in a circus. It was James Sr, who gave his son trumpet lessons at the age of 10: the youngster took to the instrument like a duck to water. A full-time career in music beckoned when James joined the Ben Pollack band in 1935 at the age of 19. James' solo work with Pollack soon impressed Goodman and it was in his band that the tall, lean James came of age as a major jazz instrumentalist. By the time that he left to front his own big-band, like fellow stars, Krupa, Hampton and Wilson, James had become one of the top virtuosi of the Swing Era.

With so much competition in the big-band field, success didn't come easy for the Harry James Orchestra, even though James had borrowed $4,500 from Goodman (in return for a one-third interest) and received further financial support from the Willard Alexander Agency. Personnel-wise, James' first outfit contained precious few outstanding soloists – apart from the

Harry James' warmth of character was such that he did not stand in Sinatra's way when the young singer wanted out.

leader himself, of course. Dave Matthews, a dependable, versatile saxophonist and arranger, was one and Jack Gardner, the band's first piano-player, was another. James, the leader, was still not quite sure whether he should concentrate on a mainly jazz-based musical policy, or whether, like others, he should attempt to accommodate non-jazzers who made up the largest potential audience. With practical considerations in mind, James must have realized the importance of including one singer at least in the band's line-up.

It was Sinatra, who became James' first male vocalist, sharing duties with dark-haired, petite Connie Haines, the replacement for Bernice Byers who left after just a few months. Trumpeter Jack Palmer handled novelty and jazzy offerings.

In the six months he spent with the band, Sinatra learned how to project his singing to different kinds of audiences at a variety of venues. He also took part in radio broadcasts and made his debut-proper on record. His wife Nancy was present for his first-ever appearance with the band at the Baltimore Hippodrome during June 1939. The new boy singer sang just two numbers: "My Love For You" and "Wishing (Will Make It So)".

Sinatra's next important appearances with the James band took place at the Roseland Ballroom, New York, during the 1939 World Fair. After one of the gigs, he received his very first notice – Sinatra had pleaded with the band manager to ask journalist George T Simon to give him a mention. Simon duly obliged. His *Metronome* review spoke of "the very pleasing vocals of Frank Sinatra, whose easy phrasing is especially commendable".

Working with James taught Sinatra about the importance of real camaraderie. There were no clashes of temperament between the sidemen, and everyone – singers and instrumentalists included – respected James, both personally and musically. Never a martinet (unlike Goodman), Harry James led by example, both on- and off-stage. A genuine friendship developed between him and his male singer that would last until the band leader's death some 44 years later.

Sinatra said "Yes" to Dorsey almost before the band-leader had popped the vital question.

When Sinatra told James he would like to accept an invitation to join the prestigious Tommy Dorsey Orchestra, it was James' warmth of character and keen understanding of the other man's ambition which led him to tear up their two-year contract.

For Dorsey, pursuit of Sinatra was a second attempt to find an adequate replacement for singer Jack Leonard, who had left in November. The "average-only" Allan DeWitt had proved a less-than-satisfactory substitute for the long-serving Leonard.

In fact, it was Leonard himself who, having heard Sinatra's "All Or Nothing At All", with James, played the record to Dorsey. Ironically, Sinatra then auditioned for the bespectacled trombonist-leader by singing Irving Berlin's "Marie" ... Leonard's most famous feature with Dorsey and one of the band's most

Happy singin',
swingin' days with
Dorsey. Frank and the
Pied Pipers in sweet
harmony. Joe
Bushkin's happy, too.

2 9 ∎

popular items. Tommy Dorsey was impressed enough to offer the job to Sinatra on the spot, along with a weekly salary cheque that was almost twice as much as the $75 James had been paying him.

Sinatra said "Yes" almost before Dorsey had popped the question. The prestige of working with such a well-known band may have been uppermost in his mind, but the increase in salary was more than welcome – especially since Nancy was pregnant.

And then there were three – Frank and Nancy with their first-born, Nancy, Jr.

With Tommy Dorsey, Sinatra's aspirations – aspirations which sometimes seemed wild and slightly ridiculous to some of his less ambitious new colleagues – could begin to take root. Musically, too, the Sinatra vocal style was about to receive enormous assistance. The leader's exceptional trombone playing, for instance, was set to deeply influence the way Sinatra controlled his breathing, which in turn would become the basis for the seamless phrasing Sinatra used so effectively on ballads.

Above all, Sinatra admired the sheer professionalism of his sometimes tetchy band leader, as well as his constant quest for musical perfection. Tommy Dorsey demanded the utmost from his men and made sure he got it. Even though singing credits on the first records were limited to the anonymous "With Vocal Refrain" – something which must have miffed Sinatra immensely – the name of the new vocalist soon became well-known to collectors of the band's recordings. Indeed, there were times when the leader came to resent the fact that Sinatra seemed to be attracting wilder applause during an evening's performance than either Dorsey himself or the band. The skinny singer held an almost uncanny fascination for the younger female members of the audience.

In the early Forties, the itinerary of a highly-successful orchestra like Dorsey's tended to be exhausting, imposing rigorous demands upon musicians. One-nighter followed one-nighter, whether the band was on tour or playing an extended season at one of the plush hotels or night-spots, where the nightly prospect of three or four – sometimes more – shows was the norm.

None of this seemed to worry Frank Sinatra, who was anxious to learn as much as possible about each area of activity in which the Dorsey outfit participated. He was quietly absorbing it all for future reference, and his knowledge of recording techniques expanded rapidly. Indeed, between February 1940 and July 1942, Sinatra appeared on 84 Tommy Dorsey titles, mostly singing solo but sometimes with the assistance of the Pied Pipers, the band's fine vocal quartet, and occasionally in tandem with Connie Haines, his erstwhile colleague with Harry James.

Sinatra's deep interest in studio work no doubt served him well when it came to a most unusual event on January 19, 1942. Although still officially an employee of Tommy Dorsey, Frank participated in his first solo recording date.

The session produced four sides, arranged and conducted by

Axel Stordahl, who had penned many of the singer's charts with the Dorsey band. Released on Bluebird, a subsidiary of Victor (the label for which the Tommy Dorsey Orchestra recorded), the four songs provided Sinatra's boss with advance warning that, sooner or later, he was going to have to look for a replacement boy singer.

And the inclusion of strings, a harp and woodwinds in the fourteen-piece accompanying ensemble showed the future direction, musically speaking, in which Sinatra was headed.

When his number one crowd-pleaser finally asked to be released from his contract in order to go solo, Tommy Dorsey turned out to be no Harry James – even though he was given the luxury of a whole year's notice. Sinatra's entreaties eventually won the day, but not before the most detailed financial and legal negotiations had been completed to the satisfaction of all parties.

First, Dorsey offered his departing vocalist $17,000 to sign a contract, which would result in Dorsey's pocketing 33 1/3 per cent of Sinatra's gross earnings over $100 for the next 10 years, plus an additional 10 per cent to the band leader's personal manager as a commission for introducing Frank Sinatra to Columbia Records. Sinatra duly signed in August 1942 but that was not the end of the matter.

Dorsey was incensed to read interviews given by Sinatra complaining bitterly at the former's financial stranglehold over him. He sued. It took until the following August for the matter to be resolved. The MCA Agency offered Dorsey $60,000. Dorsey accepted. In addition, MCA paid Dorsey $35,000 to obtain Sinatra as a client, with Sinatra himself coughing up an additional $25,000 – borrowed from Columbia's Manie Sachs – as an advance against future royalties on his Columbia recordings.

And just to top-and-tail what had by now become a real music-biz *cause celebre*, MCA agreed to split its commissions on Sinatra with GAC, with whom he had signed immediately on leaving the Dorsey band. Although Tommy Dorsey expressed satisfaction over the final arrangements, he was not at all pleased with losing not only his principal vocalist but also one of his most gifted arranging talents into the bargain. For Axel Stordahl left with Sinatra, who offered him a monthly salary considerably larger than that paid out by Dorsey ...

Las Vegas Nights: Dorsey, Rich, Elman, Connie Haines and a watchful FS (right).

RECORDS

ALTHOUGH, during the band-singing years, there was only one, rather special, occasion when Frank Sinatra actually recorded under his own name, there were many regular visits to the recording studio – especially when he was working with Tommy Dorsey's Orchestra.

The song "All Or Nothing At All" exemplified Sinatra's commitment to lyrics.

Obviously, in six months' service as Harry James' boy singer, chances to record were limited. And, frankly, the 10 different titles he cut with James, between July and November, 1939, offered hints of what was to come rather than definitive examples of Sinatra's art.

Best of the bunch were "All Or Nothing At All", "It's Funny To Everyone But Me" and "On A Little Street In Singapore" (the last-named song was revived, with success, 39 years later by the superb Manhattan Transfer vocal group).

"All Or Nothing At All" – with its near-falsetto ending – had a chequered history. On its original release, it racked up meagre sales of 8,000. Wisely, Columbia Records re-issued the side four years later when the spotlight was firmly on Sinatra, the solo performer. This time, however, the disc not only became a triumphant chart-topper but it also went on to achieve reported sales of around one million copies.

In a highly-dramatic way, it also indicated the kind of commitment the singer could bring to the lyrics of a song, an ability which was to become more and more striking over the next few years – this talent became a vital ingredient of the entire Sinatra concept.

Less dramatic, but containing their own mix of poignancy and vulnerability, were "Singapore" and "It's Funny" which likewise held out promise for the future. The remainder of Sinatra's output with the Harry James band remains primarily of historical importance. None of the other songs Sinatra was called upon to record offered much in the way of inspiration, although the 1922-published "My Buddy" still carries a kind of dated charm. All the titles listed above, including three alternative takes, are contained on the album *1935-1939: The Beginning And Harry James*.

Live recordings of Sinatra-James fare remain scarce, although in recent times several interesting airchecks have been made available on LP or CD. Taken from broadcasts dated July and August 1939, the seven Sinatra-James performances contained within *Harry James And His Orchestra: Bandstand Memories 1938 to 1948* are

basically similar to the early commercial recordings in showing Sinatra's singing ability at this early stage.

Perhaps the single most interesting aspect of these rare performances is the fact that not one of the numbers made it into the Columbia recording studios. For some reason, neither Sinatra nor James – together, or apart – ever made commercial recordings of such items as "If I Didn't Care", "Wishing" and "The Lamp Is Low". Once more, though, these excerpts of broadcasts add significantly to our knowledge of the singer's burgeoning career ...

The next stage, featuring Sinatra's considerable output as a member of the Tommy Dorsey Orchestra, still makes for absorbing listening. After six months' apprenticeship with James, this period represented the focal point of Sinatra's band-singing days, a time which saw him graduate into the ranks of polished performers, ready for his solo career.

The first Sinatra-Dorsey sessions, however, showed only a marginal improvement on the recordings with James. For instance, Sinatra's singing at the first date with Tommy Dorsey in February 1940 sounded strained. There was nothing actually wrong with his versions of "The Sky Fell Down" (significantly, arranged by Axel Stordahl) or "The Romantic" (interestingly, a new Burke-Van Heusen number, featured in *The Road To Singapore*, the latest Bob Hope/Bing Crosby movie). But there was little sign of the deep-felt emotion, which was later to become the trademark of Sinatra's singing. Nor were his great abilities as a lyric-interpreter yet in evidence.

Sinatra's keen interest in the art of recording seems to have developed during his first year with Dorsey. Session by session, there were signs of improving technique. For instance, "I'll Be

Seeing You" (from the second session, also in February) had a vocal chorus with a touching quality which few, if any, of Sinatra's band-singing rivals of the period could match. So, too, did "Polka Dots And Moonbeams" (the first Sinatra/Dorsey disc to enter the Hit Parade, albeit for a brief, one-week stay). At an April 23 date, Sinatra sounded more comfortable, accompanied on three of the five mastered titles by the Dorsey Sentimentalists, an eight-piece unit drawn from the full orchestra and featuring all-too-brief muted trumpet from the once-great, now-ailing Bunny Berigan.

The following session remains important, not only because it was the first occasion on which Frank Sinatra recorded as (temporary) lead with the Pied Pipers, but because the resulting "I'll Never Smile Again" went on to become a smash hit, spending an amazing 12 weeks as the USA's Number 1 record. By the end of the year, Sinatra-featured discs were becoming regular visitors to the Hit Parade. As his personal popularity grew and grew during 1941, the Sinatra-Dorsey hits kept coming. "Oh, Look At Me Now", co-authored by Joe Bushkin, the band's pianist, with Frank joined by Connie Haines and the Pipers, missed the top spot by one place; happily, "Dolores", also cut in January 1941, managed the feat.

In 1942, Sinatra vocals helped no fewer than 12 releases to reach the charts, with "There Are Such Things" spending six weeks in the Number 1 position. But, by the time it hit the charts (on November 7), Dorsey's premier attraction, Frank Sinatra, had been gone from the band's ranks almost two months.

Before the split, Sinatra's contributions to the Dorsey discography, between mid-1941 and up to and including his final sessions in June and July the following year, offered proof-positive of his continuing improvement.

By 1942, Sinatra's singing had become poised, assured and appealing; with specific items, such as "There Are Such Things", "In The Blue Of Evening" and "It's Always You", you could detect the emergence of a strong individual quality . In terms of control, diction and phrasing, considerable progress was clearly evident. As close inspection of the contents of *Tommy Dorsey-Frank Sinatra: The Song Is You*, confirms, Sinatra's talent had moved forward in a fascinating way.

MOVIES

Frank Sinatra's debut in movies remains shrouded in mystery. *Major Bowes' Amateur Theatre Off The Air* was the collective title for a series of shorts which were made in 1935. A 20-year-old Frank Sinatra is reported to have taken part in two or three. According to daughter Nancy, he played a waiter in the first – without being required to sing a note! – and was part of a minstrel show performance in the second.

As a member of the Dorsey band, he sang a tender "I'll Never Smile Again" in *Las Vegas Nights* (1941), a 90-minute Paramount release starring Constance Moore and Bert Wheeler among others. That brief appearance didn't make too much impact. As George T Simon noted, "[He] sings prettily in an unphotogenic manner".

Sinatra had a little more to do in *Ship Ahoy!* (1942), when he was still with Tommy Dorsey. He featured in two new numbers – "Poor You", written by E Y Harburg and Burton Lane, and "The Last Call For Love", by Harburg, Lane and Margery Cummings – then, briefly, on the standard "Moonlight Bay", assisted by the Pied Pipers.

Sinatra takes a rest while leader Tommy Dorsey serenades Constance Moore in *Ship Ahoy!*.

RADIO

From the early Forties onwards, Frank Sinatra's voice was introduced to millions of American radio listeners, who regularly checked in to broadcasts of the many big-bands of the day.

With Harry James, there was limited scope for establishing a real reputation. The comparatively few broadcasts Sinatra did make with the James band during his six-month stay nevertheless provided an opportunity for a name check nation-wide and for his voice to be introduced briefly to a large audience; see *Harry James And His Orchestra: Bandstand Memories 1938 to 1948*.

The gradual improvement in the emerging Sinatra vocal style continued throughout the Dorsey years. The best way of charting that progress is perhaps through the various airchecks which were broadcast over the years. For example, you can find some of these on the Tommy Dorsey-Frank Sinatra *The Song Is You* collection.

GIGS

From the first tentative steps with Harry James to the final band-singing days with Tommy Dorsey, Sinatra made great strides as a live performer. There was a curiously detached quality to much of Sinatra's work with James. A most important ingredient in his singing – the feel, the projection of emotion – was hardly evident in the first commercial recordings, and there wasn't much improvement with those live performances, comprising radio remotes, that have now surfaced in album form.

The outstanding live item from the James years to emerge thus far is "All Or Nothing At All" from the 1939 World Fair. Like the commercial recording of the song made the previous month in August, this was the performance above all others that gave an indication of Sinatra's potential as a vocalist with real qualities of warmth and basic communication.

An impish looking Sinatra poses with fellow Dorsey band members at the Roseland Ballroom, 1939.

Like the forgettable "Vol Vistu Gaily Star" from the same broadcast, "All Or Nothing At All" first appeared as part of *One Night Stand With Harry James, Volume II*. More recently, there has been greater access to the

They reveal a much more relaxed vocalist than the one heard on the Victor or Bluebird recordings – particularly those made during Sinatra's first year.

Certainly, the radio versions of titles such as "Who?", "Once In A While", "How Am I To Know?" and "Yearning" – none of which were recorded commercially at the time – give some kind of indication of just how well, even in 1940, Sinatra must have come across in live performance. So, too, does Frank's version of the classic Jack Leonard feature, "Marie".

Even when the material featured as part of Dorsey's *Amateur Song Writing Programme* was below par, there was no fall-off in the quality of Sinatra's singing. The same is true for albums compiled from radio collections such as *Tommy Dorsey And His Orchestra: Live At The Meadowbrook, February 11, 1941/August 18, 1942*.

Sinatra/James era with the appearance of *Harry James And His Orchestra: Bandstand Memories 1938 to 1948*. On this, you can hear the charm of the aspiring vocalist during a series of performances at the Roseland Ballroom. There are hints of better things to come from the vocals which grace such songs as "Star Dust", "My Love For You" and "This Is No Dream".

Sinatra's period with Dorsey is covered by a number of recordings now available. The Tommy Dorsey-Frank Sinatra album, *The Song Is You* offers a comprehensive retrospective of those years: it ranges from the introspective vocalizing on "Who?", "I Hear A Rhapsody", "Once In A While", or the touching "I'll Never Smile Again" (all from the singer's first year with Dorsey), to the more assured, convincing versions of "In The Blue Of Evening", "Just As Though You Were Here" and "The Song Is You" (one of Sinatra's farewell offerings), all from 1942.

There are further examples of early Dorsey-Sinatra offerings on *Sinatra: The Radio Years 1939-55*, which contains such wistfully interpreted items as "I've Got My Eyes On You", "Polka Dots And Moonbeams", "Shadows On The Sand" and "That's How It Goes".

But Sinatra the Great Lyric-Interpreter wasn't yet in full flower. That would happen when he became a fully-fledged solo artist ...

Solo Sinatra

When Frank Sinatra quit the Tommy Dorsey band in Indianapolis, on September 10, 1942, his timing, it seemed, was just about right. By then, he'd served an eminently worthwhile apprenticeship as vocalist with both the Harry James and Dorsey bands. Constant touring and playing had moulded Sinatra into a reliable performer, and he was just beginning to fulfil the great promise he had shown at the beginning of his career.

Dick Haymes – a marvellous balladeer and another big threat to Crosby.

During the four dues-paying years between 1939 and 1942, Sinatra's learning curve had been impressive and it was set to continue on an upward spiral. Year by year, he had grown in confidence – especially during the latter half of the Dorsey period. Improvement was most noticeable in the way Sinatra could project a wide variety of songs with unflappable ease – by 1942, the way he put his material across was truly convincing.

Sinatra had yet to become the legendary lyric-interpreter of later years, but there was no doubting the care he took to make even the least eloquent lyrics sound as if they contained a ring of truth. In terms of technique, control and sensitivity, Sinatra's overall method of delivery was, by 1942, beginning to impress even the Doubting Thomases among the critics, who had hitherto remained unmoved: their reviews tended to concentrate on the uninhibited reactions of adoring young female fans, who clustered round the stand during a typical Sinatra feature with Dorsey.

Sinatra – *the* classic MGM mug shot that said it all . . . Leaving Dorsey when he did was a shrewd move for another important reason – it kept Sinatra ahead of the pack. For weeks, he'd known through the big-band grapevine that rival singers Dick Haymes (his successor with both Harry James and Tommy Dorsey), Perry Como (Ted Weems), as well as Jimmy Dorsey's long-serving vocalist, Bob Eberly, were also planning to go solo. And, probably unbeknownst to the other four, Earl Hines' tall-and-handsome vocalist, Billy Eckstine, wanted to follow suit.

In fact, when granted his release from Tommy Dorsey, it was Dick Haymes, who was to prove principal threat to Sinatra's ascendancy; first, in the record charts, then as a highly-personable movie personality. Perry Como would take just a little longer to establish himself with record-buyers of the early-Forties – but not that long.

Bob Eberly, alas, would never make the big time ... even though he'd built a considerable following with the Jimmy Dorsey Orchestra, from 1936 to 1943, and had been featured on no fewer than nine chart-topping hits (two sharing credits with Helen O'Connell). Eberly's early popularity had brought him third place among the top pop vocalists in the annual *Billboard* college polls, between 1940 and 1943, but his career proper was interrupted by military service. Even though he wangled himself a posting to Chicago, where he worked with an orchestra fronted by (Captain) Wayne King, following discharge, he never fully established himself as a big name solo performer. Eberly's post-war career ran to a trio of minor hit recordings, leadership for a while of his own big bands and appearances (sometimes reunited with O'Connell) at nostalgia-based concerts.

Career-wise, Billy Eckstine's development took much longer than the others, due to his whole-hearted commitment to fronting a legendary jazz orchestra. This has since been recognized as one of the most exciting outfits in the whole of big-band jazz history: the

band was the crucible for a whole, new and revolutionary kind of jazz called either bebop or rebop; ultimately, simply bop.

The doubly talented Billy Eckstine, band leader-cum-balladeer.

Band membership comprised many future giants of the genre, including, at various times, such luminaries as Charlie Parker, Dizzy Gillespie, Fats Navarro, Dexter Gordon, Sonny Stitt, Gene Ammons and the ever-present Art Blakey. Sarah Vaughan shared vocals with leader Eckstine – but it was his more-or-less straight ballad-singing which achieved any kind of commercial viability for this remarkable unit. These musicians were light years ahead of their time and just what the ballroom types, who normally followed Glenn Miller and the Dorseys, – let alone fans of the Mickey Mouse bands like King, Sammy Kaye and Kyser! – made of them is almost beyond comprehension. That the band lasted for as long as it did

One black vocalist was receiving ever-increasing acceptance at this time – namely, Nat King Cole. Singing was just one part of his talents: to the jazz-minded, he was one of the music's most gifted and influential keyboard players; for others, his personal appeal lay within the context of the King Cole Trio, whose repertoire – an important aspect of the combo's growing popularity – included a crowd-pleasing mix of standards and current ballads, jump tunes, R&B originals, novelties ... and an acceptable form of basic jazz that was scarcely likely to offend the non-jazzers. But Nat King Cole's reputation as a major solo singer was not to be consolidated until the end of the Forties. That was when he disbanded the Trio in exchange for a less jazz-based band, designed to give his recordings a bigger sound ...

The Nat King Cole Trio.

(1944-47) was due entirely to Eckstine's dedication; even before the inevitable crunch came, he was up to his neck in personal debt.

Even without the numerous near-disasters that dogged his bandleading career, it is impossible to say whether Eckstine on his own could have competed with the likes of Sinatra and Dick Haymes. The truth is that Eckstine would have been one of precious few black solo vocalists to venture into what was then a white-oriented world of popular entertainment. And, with the exception of a small handful of performers (e.g. Duke Ellington, Louis Armstrong, Ethel Waters and Cab Calloway), the prospects for black super-stardom during this period were distinctly unpromising.

For Frank Sinatra, though, the future looked full of promise.

With Hollywood beckoning and radio still a potent medium, a major problem arose with recording plans.

For one thing, he had eyes for Hollywood and wanted to conquer the silver screen. He had also become increasingly aware of the importance of radio, and his ambitions were no longer limited to guest-spot appearances on

other people's programmes – he wanted a regular show of his own.

Supreme confidence in his own ability – a confidence bordering on outright arrogance – gave him every reason to believe that, sooner rather than later, he would be accorded his own sponsored radio series: one that would rival Bing Crosby's widely-popular *Kraft Music Hall* series, which had been continually on the air since 1935. Thanks to the brash and cocky mentality, which had helped him survive two and a half years of non-stop singing with the Tommy Dorsey Band, there was little or no doubt in Sinatra's mind that he would soon be recognized as the world's leading vocal performer, both in concert and on the nightclub scene.

However, a major problem arose in a crucial area which held up Sinatra and his rivals for a long time. On August 1, 1942, following a dispute over musicians' royalty payments and through the unstinting efforts of its ruthless, much-feared president, James Petrillo, the powerful American Federation of Musicians instituted a blanket ban on recording activities by musicians. Singers, however, were allowed to record – even though they could only perform in a strictly solo capacity or, alternatively, utilize the services of an established vocal group or specially-assembled chorus. For Sinatra, Columbia chose the latter.

A strike ensued and remained solid, with neither side willing to make concessions. The dispute finished, to all intents and purposes, some thirteen months later when the union came to an agreement through Petrillo and his officers that satisfied all the record companies, except the two largest: Victor and Columbia. They held out for a further 14 months before they too agreed terms and contracts were signed on November 11, 1944.

Sinatra must have been particularly upset because, thanks to the personal intercession of the company's chief A&R man, Manie Sachs, he had chosen to sign with Columbia after leaving Dorsey: Sachs had continued to be impressed with Sinatra's progress, since first hearing him on-stage over a year before the split. He and Sinatra were to become good friends and, under Sachs' wise guidance, the Columbia association started well – despite the fact that Frank Sinatra was not allowed to employ the services of the man who was to be his closest and most important musical associate for the next ten years. At least, though, Axel Stordahl's brilliant conducting and arranging skills could still enhance Sinatra's singing on radio and in Hollywood movies during the period of the AFM

All-star radio: Django Reinhardt, Claudette Colbert, Frank, Bing, at the Hollywood Canteen, 1945.

ban. Sachs' influence and judgement would continue until 1950, when he left to join Victor. But the personal friendship lasted until the A&R man's death in 1959 at the age of just 53.

After Frank Sinatra split from the Dorsey band in 1942, he went to the West Coast to check out Hollywood and his prospects in motion pictures. As pianist-arranger-bandleader Skitch Henderson told journalist George T Simon, Sinatra had visions of landing a staff singing post at NBC in the movie capital.

There was, however, to be no NBC post. Instead, Sinatra was drafted into the cast of the movie, *Reveille With Beverly*, a run-of-the-mill production from Columbia Pictures. The movie was little more than an excuse to parade the musical talents of top bands (Duke Ellington, Count Basie, Bob Crosby and Freddie Slack), vocalists (apart from Sinatra, Ella Mae Morse and the Mills Brothers) and the impressive terpsichorean skills of dancer Ann

Miller. Surrounded by a bevy of Hollywood lovelies, Sinatra sang a poised, sincerely-felt "Night And Day". Being the briefest of movie debuts, though, his was scarcely a riveting performance.

Sinatra soon returned to New York, where, thanks to Manie Sachs, he joined the list of clients at the powerful GAC agency. To pay the bills, he did a CBS radio show for five months, starting in October. This, in turn, led to involvement with the Lucky Strike-sponsored *Your Hit Parade*, which began in February 1943.

But it was a remarkable series of gigs which brought Sinatra's biggest breakthrough... remarkable as much for the way the audience went wild as for any brilliance on the part of the singer. Again, it was Manie Sachs, who engineered things. He obtained a booking for Frank at the Mosque Theater, a large hall of entertainment in Newark, New Jersey. Then, Sachs invited along Bob Weitman, the managing director of the prestigious Paramount Theater. Impressed as he was by Sinatra's singing, Weitman was astounded by the near-hysterical reaction of the predominantly youthful audience.

The very next day, Weitman called Benny Goodman, who was the headline act at the Paramount, and told him that he was attaching Frank Sinatra as an "extra added attraction" to the bill. Goodman's only comment was: "Who's he?" The King of Swing was soon to find out. But, for the opening show on December 30, 1942, Goodman confined himself to introducing the newcomer in a way that was brief and to the point,

"And now, Frank Sinatra ..."

The "that" to which Goodman referred with such genuine incredulity was, of course, the "official" opening of the Bobbysox Era. It was also the beginning of an amazing period in Sinatra's eventful show business career, when mass adulation – particularly from young women but by no means restricted to one gender – reached its first peak.

Benny sings Sinatra, Frank plays Goodman – the two giants have fun on Sinatra's radio show.

Even before the young singer stepped on-stage, the roar of anticipation from the teenage audience was deafening. Both Sinatra and Goodman stood rooted to the spot as if paralyzed.

First to recover, the bandleader turned around, faced the perpetrators of the noise and inquired of no-one in particular, "What the fuck is that?" Sinatra laughed, relaxed and ambled his way out to centre-stage. Following this, he gave what George T Simon later described as a "tremendously effective show".

Frankie! For the grown-ups he was hardly a Gable, Taylor or Power. But for the bobby-soxers, he was IT!

Measured against previous outbreaks of mass hero-worship in the US, this kind of uninhibited fan frenzy far outstripped anything previously accorded to matinee idols Rudolph Valentino and Rudy Vallee (even allowing for the fact that, generally speaking, the age group of those idolaters made them rather more grown-up). This kind of adulation – the tears, the fainting, the screams – was not to be seen again until the arrival on the pop scene at the beginning of the Fifties of the Nabob of Sob, Johnny Ray.

Later, pop idols such as Elvis Presley, the Beatles, the Rolling Stones and teenyboppers, such as David Cassidy, the Osmonds (individually and collectively) and the Jackson Five, exerted the same near-hypnotic effect on predominantly teenage admirers. In more recent times, Michael Jackson, Prince and Madonna have elicited the same kind of reaction from literally millions of their faithful flock, worldwide.

After this sensational opening, Sinatra and Goodman continued in tandem for the rest of the one-month booking. Weitman was so utterly delighted with Sinatra's Paramount debut that he offered the new Number One vocal heart-throb a further month's appearances immediately after the first batch was completed. It took the eager Sinatra seconds to say "Yes". During the second month, accompaniment was provided by the orchestras of Sonny Dunham and Johnny Long. Meanwhile, Goodman, complete with Orchestra and Sextet, plus young blonde vocalist Peggy Lee, had departed to fulfil previous engagements.

Critic George T Simon had followed Sinatra's progress throughout the band-singing period, and so it came as no surprise when he put in an appearance at the Sinatra-Goodman season. His review was enthusiastic. "He could have stayed on indefinitely, but he didn't..." And, continued Simon, the most memorable individual performance of the evening was his tender version of "She's Funny That Way", the Richard Whiting-Neil Moret classic published in 1928, which Sinatra had probably heard sung by Billie Holiday on 52nd Street. At the Paramount, he was supported only by Goodman's pianist, Jess Stacy, a simple

set-up that was to become a Sinatra trademark in live performance for the rest of his career.

As Sinatra's extended season at the Paramount continued and the crowds grew larger, the adolescent screams and shrieks grew louder and more insistent. Weitman engaged extra guards to maintain order. Even then, some girls refused to leave their seats after the show, insisting on remaining where they were until the following morning. Some fainted – either from the excitement of seeing their hero on-stage, or from hunger because they hadn't been able to eat!

Many people remained unmoved by the furore surrounding Sinatra. They found it difficult to understand what such a large percentage of teenage America saw in the thin, gangling Frank Sinatra of the bobbysox days; even today, there are those who still cannot relate to any of the explanations given.

The way they saw it, Sinatra was hardly in the same league as movie heart-throbs of the early-Forties – Gable, Taylor, Power et al. In their eyes, he seriously lacked machismo. And the sometimes limp-fitting suits he wore, the floppy bow-ties and the tousled hair that occasionally fell over his forehead, together hardly seemed to add up to Sinatra the Sex Symbol.

But sex symbol Sinatra was, without a doubt. On-stage, he possessed an indefinable kind of magnetism that was apparent even to certain grown-ups, who, out of perverse curiosity, turned up at his concerts. Cool, confident Sinatra certainly knew how to play up his sexual side in the way he moved, and how to seduce the audience with a sudden intake of breath, or a smile, or by a deliberate gesture with a free hand. His voice was sexy, too. Time and again, he would bring increased screams and shouts from his audiences by deliberately extending a single word, or stressing a certain phrase: "I'm not much to look at, nothin' to see ...", from "She's Funny That Way", inevitably brought forth a torrent of protests, in the vein of

"No-o-o, Frankie-ee! You're gorgeous ... You're super ..."

Reviewers, who deigned to attend a Sinatra performance, tended not to agree that Frankie was gorgeous. Invariably, few words were wasted on Sinatra's actual singing; instead, reviews concentrated on deprecating the star's negative influence on youngsters, as well as deploring the manner in which he could manipulate their emotions. Needless to say, there were few kind words for his mode of dress either. But one publication at least conceded that, in the flesh, Sinatra possessed charisma. A reviewer for *Time* magazine declared,

"Not since Rudolph Valentino has American womanhood made such unabashed public love to an entertainer."

The new king of the nightclub singers. Sinatra won over even the hardest-to-please audience, and silenced the noisiest drunk.

After the successful launch of his Lucky Strike-sponsored radio show in February 1943, came Sinatra's first involvement with the night-club circuit, an area where he would find few, if any, rivals in succeeding years ... let alone anyone to surpass him.

On March 17, Sinatra began a season at the Riobamba Club, located on West 57th Street, Manhattan. Originally pencilled in as second string to veteran comedian Walter O'Keefe, Frank Sinatra was an instant smash hit. Not only did he produce top-quality singing, but he also continued to pack in customers during a four-week engagement. Night after night, the reaction of the Riobamba audiences was genuinely enthusiastic. So pleased was the club's manager that the original weekly fee of $750 was hiked to $1,000, well before the month had been completed. By the time the season had been extended – and then re-extended – that weekly figure had risen by another $500.

After the Riobamba triumph, Sinatra was booked into Frank Dailey's Meadowbrook nightspot. Once again, he scored with SRO (Sold Right Out) audiences, some of whom had come along specifically to mock this skinny young man – who looked much younger than his 28 years – and put him in his place. Then, in May, came a return to the Paramount. And now his weekly salary had risen from $2,100 to a princely $3,100 ...

By the fall, Frank Sinatra was appearing in the plush Wedgwood Room at the distinctly upmarket Waldorf-Astoria, New York. Now, there could be no doubt whatsoever that he had truly hit the big time. The only negative moment of the Waldorf-Astoria season came one evening, when an obviously drunk customer lurched to his feet and bawled out loudly, "You stink!" Stopping in mid-song, Frank strode purposefully from the stage and invited the drunk outside. The offer was refused, without a word being offered in reply.

Returning to the stage, Sinatra addressed the audience. "Ladies and gentlemen, I like to sing. I'm paid to sing. Those who don't like my voice are not compelled to come and surely are under no obligation to stay." There was spontaneous applause.

That Sinatra could perform just as impressively outdoors had been confirmed almost two months before the Wedgwood Room gig.

On August 14, 1943, he succeeded in packing the Hollywood Bowl on his first appearance there. Morris Stoloff, the film

Frank signs for the fans at a Red Cross fundraising event at Ebbetsfield in 1944.

composer-arranger, conducted for him. And Sinatra was astonished by the volume, as well as the genuine warmth, of applause he received from a capacity audience of West Coast fans.

To all but those without ears to hear, there was no doubt that Sinatra was now a superb singer.

But even more extraordinary fan-reaction was to follow in October 1944, after the announcement of a further Paramount booking: this time, the tumultuous reception was not confined within any one venue. It all started when Sinatra arrived for a 6 am rehearsal on the first day of the engagement and was startled to observe almost a thousand bobbysox girls waiting outside the theatre. Despite a 9 pm curfew for juveniles – imposed by Mayor LaGuardia – police maintained that queues had begun to form at three in the morning. By seven, the main queue stretched down to Eighth Avenue. When the theatre opened at 8.30 am, all 3,600 seats were filled.

A new movie – *Our Hearts Were Young And Gay*, starring Gail Russell, Diana Lynn, Charles Ruggles and Dorothy Gish – which preceded the Sinatra appearance, backed by the Raymond Paige Orchestra, was completely ignored. The bobbysoxers chatted and chanted their hero's name throughout its duration. When, finally, he appeared, all hell was let loose.

The next day – Columbus Day and a school holiday to boot – saw even more amazing scenes. Approximately 10,000 youngsters queued six-abreast outside the auditorium, with another huge crowd, estimated at 20,000, jamming Times Square. There were numerous fainting incidents, some injuries, minor vandalism – and several arrests. Vast numbers of police reinforcements were called in to control these remarkable scenes. Even so, they were easily outnumbered and absolutely powerless to do anything about dispersing the crowd.

Inside the Paramount, hundreds of young girls refused to leave their seats after the first show – some managed to stay for two, or even three, performances. And such was the ferocity of their adulation that, on the third day, an 18-year-old boy was almost lynched by a gang of incensed females, after he'd thrown an egg with admirable accuracy at Sinatra during his rendition of "I Don't Know Why". On stage, Sinatra himself had to be protected from the attentions of his rabid fans. Their single-minded attempts to claw at his hair, clothes or bow-ties required

the combined energy of the law and his own personal bodyguards to prevent physical damage.

The bobbysox phenomenon lasted for several years. During that time, it succeeded in dividing the young from the old. Many thousands of words were written by journalists, music critics, the clergy and even leading psychoanalysts in all manner of publications to explain the "problem". The explanations given were numerous and wildly differing, sometimes bizarre. For some medical pundits, it was due to "war-time degeneracy", to others it was all "a product of the maternal urge to feed the hungry".

There was also much media speculation about the causes of such extraordinary events as "The Columbus Day Riot", as the incident henceforth became known, and how much it was down to the natural (or even unnatural) instincts of pubescence. But here most commentators were overlooking the exceptional PR skills of one George B Evans ...

George B Evans became Frank Sinatra's press agent in 1942. During the next six years, he made himself absolutely indispensable to the singer in keeping the name "Sinatra" on every front page – and, just as importantly, defending the star against numerous press attacks on his character.

Many of these accusations appear to have been well-founded. It was Evans, for instance, who worked wonders in muting the possibility of the worst kind of personal publicity. This followed a succession of extra-marital affairs that threatened to blow apart Sinatra's cleancut-family-man image, which the PR man constantly stressed in his hand-outs and personal conversations with newspaper journalists. It was Evans' skill, too, that helped reduce the publicity which automatically surrounded Sinatra's outbursts in public – often violent outbursts – which were invariably aimed at reporters and photographers. And, of course, in the first place, it had been Evans, whose untiring efforts helped ignite the bobbysox phenomenon, then continued to fan the flames of publicity, which inevitably led to the Columbus Day episode.

Despite continued scepticism in some quarters of the critical fraternity, Sinatra's vocal talent endured.

In a strictly PR context, Evans' greatest achievements surrounded events at the Paramount Theater. No doubt of that. His highly-imaginative scams involved not only whipping up frenzy among scores of teenage girls, but manipulation of Sinatra himself. For example, Evans suggested to Sinatra that caressing the microphone (the stand-up variety) would elicit an excited response from young women in the audience. So, too, would the occasional swaying of the slim frame, with or without mike.

If Sinatra held his arms wide open, when he sang the phrase

"Come to Papa, come to Papa, do ..."

from the Gershwin standard, "Embraceable You", it would bring front-row teenyboppers to yell, "Oh, Daddy!", the reply which Evans had planted earlier. A little further coaching from Evans induced some girls to faint, and others to moan loudly.

Frank Sinatra with Ava Gardner, an affair that went the whole distance, into marriage.

Ever the perfectionist, Frank took
concert rehearsals seriously – as at
Lewisohn, NYC (far left) and the
Hollywood Bowl, California (left).

On Columbus Day, a school holiday, Evans gave away hundreds of free tickets for the Paramount shows. Nevertheless, later, he always fiercely denied stage-managing subsequent events in the street outside the Paramount Theater. However, he never denied sweet-talking the leading booking agency for the nation's symphony orchestras into allowing his client to play a series of concerts – at Lewisohn Stadium, New York, the Hollywood Bowl and at Washington, DC, utilizing four leading classical ensembles – so that those venues' poor box-office receipts would be given a much-needed financial boost.

Although heavy press criticism of events surrounding Sinatra's personal performances tended to overshadow other professional commitments, Frank Sinatra was still making his name as a recording artist. Despite the absence of arranger Axel Stordahl, the first five *a cappella* studio sessions – held in New York, between June and November 1943 – demonstrated yet again that the decision to go it alone was the right one.

With Alec Wilder providing high-quality choral arrangements – and no doubt adding words of wisdom to an anxious Sinatra – and the backgrounds handled with predictable expertise by a selection of top session vocalists, led by Bobby Tucker, the results, from Sinatra's standpoint, were promising.

Even though there were moments when his singing tended to lack total conviction, there was no doubt that Sinatra was hitting the spot in terms of sincerity, sensitivity and musicality. His approach to lyrics showed an attention to detail that would become part-and-parcel of his future recording work. The diction was faultless. The phrasing was elegant. The control very good. And there was no lacking in feel – even though the depth of expression had yet to reach the level of his Columbia recordings from 1944 and thereafter ... and, of course, which Sinatra raised to optimum level in his post-Columbia years.

In terms of artistic development, Sinatra's work as a recording artist stayed well ahead of his career in films. The same can be said of his rapid growth as a live performer.

As far as Hollywood was concerned, the studios didn't care about the quality of characters Sinatra had to play on-screen during his first five years – inevitably, they would be the warm-smiling, likeable type. Naturally, in the film companies' eyes, Sinatra was first and foremost a singer. However, no matter what kind of nonsensical story or setting was involved, there was thankfully scope for The Voice to deliver the goods. And, usually, Sinatra was well-served by the material written for his movies, which he made initially for RKO, then MGM (after signing a highly lucrative contract with the latter).

Frank's radio series presented talents like the delicious young Jane Powell.

Harold Adamson and Jimmy McHugh were the songwriters for *Higher And Higher*, Sinatra's first full-length motion picture. For *Step Lively*, the team of Sammy Cahn and Jule Styne was brought in to produce new material. Between 1943 and 1951, the same combination of talents was involved in *Anchors Aweigh!*, *It Happened In Brooklyn* and *Double Dynamite*. Film critics gave a collective thumbs-up to the on-screen vocals – albeit, in some cases, grudgingly – but few were over-impressed by Sinatra's potential in the acting stakes.

Sinatra's progress in conquering the US airwaves ran parallel with his successes on record. The most important, early developments in these vital areas related to his obtaining top billing on the prestigious *Your Hit Parade* radio series (which he contributed to for two separate runs) and, finally his very own series, *Songs By Sinatra*.

Both on radio and on record, his work was of consistent high quality. And there were few, if any, complaints about his concert or club appearances. Whether performing at the Hollywood Bowl or at the Waldorf-Astoria, Sinatra's stature as an artist kept growing throughout the Forties and, well before the decade was out, he was acknowledged as king of the live performers.

Towards the end of the Forties, though, a noticeable decline set in. His often tempestuous personal private life didn't help. Still less did his torrid romance with Ava Gardner, known to magazine readers as the Most Beautiful Woman In The World. While this affair was going on, the gradual disintegration of his marriage with Nancy gave the press ample opportunity to put Sinatra's life under the microscope.

Perhaps foolishly, Sinatra gave them plenty of ammunition with which to bombard his personal reputation. The attacks and counter-attacks continued accelerating alarmingly as members of the press from all over the world pursued Sinatra and Gardner relentlessly, wherever they went.

Sinatra's popularity slumped disastrously and this was reflected by a marked decrease in sales of his records. Reviews, too, were often less kind than hitherto. Ratings for the *Light Up Time* radio series began to worry its sponsors. By the beginning of 1952, there were rumours that the days of *The Frank Sinatra Show*, on television, were numbered. And the movies weren't pulling in the punters as before ...

Every picture tells a story ... A dejected Frank Sinatra stares into space.

Already, some critics were sharpening their knives. The obituaries were being prepared.

1943-1952

RECORDS

FROM HIS VERY FIRST solo Columbia recordings, it was obvious that Sinatra was ready to launch himself as a vocalist in his own right.

True, there was an occasional hesitancy in those first *a cappella* sessions, but this could no doubt be put down to the absence of Axel Stordahl's arranging skills – the American Federation of Musicians had banned musicians from taking part in recording until a new agreement over royalties was reached. Even so, composer and arranger Alec Wilder had coached up the mixed chorus into performing excellently as surrogate background in place of the band.

Even at this early stage in his career, Sinatra was something of a perfectionist inside a recording studio. This is perhaps best illustrated by the fact that he cut three separate versions of "People Will Say We're In Love" before, finally, he was satisfied. Two versions were also made of "The Music Stopped". In this **Rehearsals don't** case, however, both takes were to **always have to be a** remain on the shelf until the Sixties, **drag.** before they received a first-time release. Whatever misgivings there may have been about accompaniments, Sinatra's new recordings sold in large numbers. Even though Dick Haymes copped top spot on the Hit Parade with "You'll Never Know", Sinatra took the same song to Number 2; "People Will Say We're In Love" peaked at 3; "Couldn't Sleep A Wink Last Night" at 4; "Sunday, Monday, Or Always" at 9; and "Lovely Way To Spend An Evening" failed by just one place to make the Top 10.

At all five of the all-ballad *a cappella* sessions, there was a high level of artistic consistency in Sinatra's vocals, which augured well for recordings once the union ban was over. With Stordahl finally in harness, further improvement seemed guaranteed. And that's how it went at the very next Columbia session, almost exactly one year after the final date with Wilder and the Bobby Tucker Singers.

Backed by a 35-piece orchestra including nineteen strings (and featuring a harp), there was a real authority to Sinatra's singing. Stordahl's writing was exquisite – as it remained throughout most of

the Columbia years. Together with a beautifully-felt version of "White Christmas" (which made it to the Top 10), Sinatra's first rhythmic excursion on record still sounds pretty good. The recording of "Saturday Night (Is The Loneliest Night of the Week)" proved irresistible to his fans and, like "You'll Never Know", only missed out being Sinatra's first chart-topper by one place.

When you listen to the magnificent 1993-released 12-CD boxed set, *Frank Sinatra: The Complete Columbia Recordings, 1943-1952*, the level of vocal performance – thanks, of course, to the presence of Stordahl – is excellent proof not only of Sinatra's consistency, but also of the fact that he continued to set higher and higher standards for other singers to keep up with.

In the whole, wide field of popular music, Sinatra was the greatest vocal performer of his era – even allowing for the fact that Crosby never sounded better than during the Forties, or that Haymes, Como and Eckstine were likewise coming into their prime.

During this period, Sinatra recorded prolifically, yet, time and again, managed to turn out absolute gems. It would be tedious to mention them all, but the list of classics must include "Mam'selle" (the last of three Hit Parade Number 1 successes), "White Christmas", "Nancy", "Ol' Man River", "Embraceable You" (in many ways, the archetypal Frank Sinatra song of the Forties), "She's Funny That Way", "Where Or When", "The Things We Did Last Summer"; a two-part "Soliloquy", from *Carousel* (his first solo 12-inch disc release); "Time After Time", "Always", "But Beautiful", "I've Got A Crush On You" (with sensitive trumpet obbligato/solo from Bobby Hackett) and "Why Was I Born?"

There were other outstanding delights around this time, including a one-off jazz date as a member of the 1946 Metronome All Stars (who included Coleman Hawkins, Johnny Hodges, Nat Cole and Buddy Rich), with Sinatra taking a chorus-and-half of "Sweet Lorraine" in appropriate loose-swinging fashion. Another one-off delight featured a duet with the legendary Pearl Bailey ("A Little Learnin' Is A Dangerous Thing"). Sinatra handled his part – repartee and all – remarkably well in such formidable company.

In more conventional mode, Sinatra's finest individual moments came on July 30, 1945. Sinatra empathized brilliantly with

his collaborator, Axel Stordahl, who had produced some of his most sensitive writing for a nine-piece chamber-style ensemble with just three strings. His phrasing and feel on "Someone To Watch Over Me", "These Foolish Things" and "I Don't Know Why" are well-nigh flawless. Pride of place, however, goes to the definitive treatment of "You Go To My Head", which is as near to perfection, vocally and instrumentally, as you could ever get.

The post-1947 Columbia work tends to show not only a slow decline in Sinatra's vocal powers, but also reflects the myriad of personal and professional problems – sometimes quite vividly.

Most revealing is his first recording of "I'm A Fool To Want You" (with Sinatra sharing lyric-writing credits with composers Jack Wolf and Joel Herron). George T Simon has called it "the most moving side Sinatra has ever recorded". Certainly, even today it sounds like a genuine *cri de coeur* to Ava Gardner. In its own way, Sinatra's revival of "Love Me", first published in 1934 and recorded at the same date, imparts the same kind of message but, this time, delivered strictly *sotto voce*.

These last two songs were made during the infamous Mitch Miller period – Miller took over from Manie Sachs as A&R man at Columbia. So, even if the gimmicks and totally inappropriate material of this time tend to be remembered most of all, Miller did at least supervize one session which produced worthwhile Sinatra material. Perhaps the worst example of "Mitch Millerism" was the excruciating "Mama Will Bark", with the busty European cabaret artist Dagmar contributing nothing towards a thoroughly disastrous concoction, even with studio man Donald Bain's authentic canine noises in the background.

MOVIES

BY THE MID-FORTIES, Sinatra had become one of the top box-office draws in Hollywood. True, there was very little to suggest any particular acting ability, simply because none of the roles he took on demanded it. Sinatra was in movies because of his huge popularity ... and to provide songs.

After the all too brief appearance in *Reveille with Beverly*, came Sinatra's debut proper in RKO's *Higher And Higher*, which was freely adapted from a Broadway musical of the same name. Sinatra played Glen, the aspiring playwright – a nice, friendly, rather naive young man, exuding an appealing boy-next-door charm ... exactly the kind of personality, which he would reproduce for most of his Forties motion picture appearances.

Simply because of Sinatra's image, off-screen as well as on, many film critics were ready to pounce on the star but only the most hard-bitten and churlish could fail to be delighted by his singing. In *Higher And Higher*, Sinatra was well-served by the talents of songsmiths Harold Adamson and Jimmy McHugh. Effortless ease is apparent in the way he projects each of the three most important songs ("I Couldn't Sleep A Wink Last Night"; "Lovely Way To Spend An Evening"; "The Music Stopped"). And there is no lack of warmth.

Step Lively (RKO, 1945), with songwriters Cahn & Styne producing their first collective efforts on his behalf, was more or less a repeat performance. No commercial recordings were made of the likes of "Come Out, Come Out, Wherever You Are", or "Some Other Time" (arguably, the best), although V-Disc versions now exist in CD format [The "'V-Discs': The Columbia Years 1943-1952"].

The full-frontal Sinatra – the one presented to millions who flocked to see his Forties' movies.

"Wanna make a kiss-call?" asks Anne Jeffreys in *Step Lively*. Frank keeps quiet.

Sinatra and Kelly – the regular MGM sailor-boy duo of the Forties. All singin', all dancin' – romance and fun, too. This one's *Anchors Aweigh!*, a blockbuster from 1945.

Anchors Aweigh! (MGM,1945) has even finer Sinatra vocals. It was his first high-profile movie – the first of three he would make with Gene Kelly and his first in sailor-boy suit, but the third with Stordahl's unmistakable vocal arrangements - and everyone came out of it well, including Sinatra. Vocally, he sounded more assured and convincing than ever. Cahn & Styne had come up with five more numbers, including a particularly appealing Sinatra-Gene Kelly duet ("I Begged Her"). Finest of the quintet, though, were a tender "The Charm Of You" and, in particular, a yearning rendition of "I Fall In Love Too Easily", with Sinatra seated in front of a grand piano on-stage at an empty Hollywood Bowl.

The 10 minute-long *The House I Live In* (RKO, 1945) received a Special Award from the Academy of Motion Picture Arts And Sciences for its plea for racial tolerance, a message that Sinatra delivered with sincerity and no Hollywood-type falsehood. Musically, he handled "If You Are But A Dream" and the heavily patriotic "The House I Live In" with a similar lack of melodrama. The critics were impressed.

If only they'd closed their eyes, they might have appreciated just how impressive a job Sinatra made of "Ol' Man River" – used as the climax of *Till The Clouds Roll By* (1946), MGM's star-studded Jerome Kern biopic. Unfortunately, the image of Frank Sinatra, clad all in white, perched atop a white dais and surrounded by an all-white orchestra and chorus, stands forever as Hollywood at its bad-taste worst.

It Happened In Brooklyn (MGM, 1946) found Sinatra switching from navy-blue to khaki to play a GI returning home from war. His acting at last gave hints of a promising, if underdeveloped, talent – helped unquestionably by the presence of Jimmy Durante alongside him. But the singing still took centre stage.

A duet between Sinatra and Durante, "The Song's Gotta Come From The Heart", remains a delightful excursion into vaudeville. It was just one of five new Cahn-Styne creations, which included Sinatra on his own sounding wistful on "It's The Same Old Dream", happy-go-lucky on "I Believe" and especially persuasive with "Time After Time". Less important are a tentative stab at Mozart, "La Ci Darem La Mano" – a typical "touch

Higher and Higher: Glen – nice friendly young man exuding appealing boy-next-door charm.

of class", Hollywood-style – and Sinatra's version of the traditional "Black Eyes", sung in his own special brand of Russian.

A few more song writing contributions from Cahn and Styne might have made *The Miracle Of The Bells* (RKO, 1948) a tad more bearable. This strictly non-musical non-event had Sinatra donning clerical garb as a Roman Catholic priest with but one song to perform. It was another imported number, "Ever Homeward" – anglicized by Cahn, polished by Styne –

Sinatra impressed the critics as well as his fans with *The House I Live In*.

sung in both its original Polish and English. But as for acting, there was nothing to write home about ...

Sinatra's only role of note came in the film that book-ended the decade: *Meet Danny Wilson* (Universal International, 1951). Even so, the movie was primarily a musical with Sinatra more or less playing himself. The plot was traditional: a singer, who is trying to make it, is befriended then stitched up by a racketeer night-club owner. There were more songs than Sinatra had sung in any previous movie, all but one standards. These included "She's Funny That Way", "How Deep Is The Ocean?", "That Old Black Magic" and "I've Got A Crush On You" ... and they betrayed little trace of any decline in Sinatra's vocal powers.

In between *Miracle Of The Bells* and *Meet Danny Wilson* was sandwiched a diverse selection of average-to-good, poor and downright terrible films. Most definitely in the latter category was the excruciating *The Kissing Bandit* (MGM, 1948), about which nothing further need be said.

Take Me Out To The Ball Game (MGM, 1949) was a reunion with Gene Kelly and concerned a couple of vaudevillians, who also excel at baseball. Although directed by the legendary Busby Berkeley, it failed to take off. All but two numbers have Sinatra sharing vocals with Kelly and co-stars Betty Garrett, Jules Munshin and Esther Williams. Sung alone, "She's The Right Girl for Me" is pure Sinatra. Regrettably, "Boys And Girls Like You And Me" was left on the cutting room floor. For years, copies of the soundtrack version of this number have circulated among collectors. However, the laser disc version of *That's Entertainment* includes the missing sequence – which was apparently found only in 1993 – in all its glory ...

On The Town – classic Hollywood, classic Sinatra and Kelly.

Double Dynamite (RKO, 1951) is a touch better than *The Kissing Bandit* but that isn't saying a lot. Even the usually enlivening presence of Groucho Marx can scarcely inject life into this Irving Cummings-directed flop. Messrs Cahn and Styne produced two of their least effective numbers, which Sinatra performed efficiently, in duet with Marx on "It's Only Money" and with Jane Russell on "Kisses And Tears". Sinatra actually recorded the last-named song twice – first as a solo performance (1949), then with Russell and the Modernaires (1950).

Take Me Out To The Ball Game – Sinatra, Gene Kelly, Esther Williams and Betty Garrett.

Of all the Sinatra musicals of the Forties the one that will be remembered most fondly is MGM's classic *On The Town* (1949). It was to be Sinatra's last collaboration with Gene Kelly (who co-directed with Stanley Donen) and it also reunited him with Garrett and Munshin from *Take Me Out To The Ball Game*. Sinatra's overall performance matched the rest of the cast in terms of exuberance and sheer *joie de vivre*. Once again, he was cast as the hapless if likeable sailor, who nevertheless finds romance (with Garrett, a wisecracking New York taxi-driver). Sinatra shared the song allocation with the other leading characters in various permutations, including the spirited opening "New York, New York", "Count On Me" and the title tune. Best of all, though, is "You're Awful" a charming duet with Garrett.

RADIO

SINATRA'S GROWING STATURE in the field of radio matched his success in live performance and the encouraging sales of his first solo recordings. Of course, radio could never hope to equal the glamour of the silver screen, or be as accessible as the gramophone record in the purchaser's home and heart. Nevertheless, radio was a powerful medium for any performer and Sinatra was fortunate to be given many opportunities to parade his talent on the airwaves throughout the next five years and beyond.

There were many guest appearances on shows, which catered for huge audiences such as *Here's To The Veterans*, *Personal Album*, *Mail Call* and *Something For The Girls* – many of these were transcribed and re-broadcast by the Armed Forces Radio Service. The AFRS also produced its own series of radio specials. The most widely-regarded of these was *Command Performance*. Frank Sinatra became a regular and welcome guest on this latter presentation.

Most important of all for Sinatra, during his first year away from Dorsey, was to take over the coveted male-vocalist spot on *Your Hit Parade*, networked by CBS and sponsored by Lucky Strike Cigarettes. It was the most popular series of its kind, a forerunner to many future similar shows around the world.

Bob Hope and Frank Sinatra relaxing at a radio rehearsal.

During 1943, Sinatra commenced his own series, *The Broadway Bandbox*, followed in 1944 by a short-lived series The *Frank Sinatra Programme*, sponsored by Vimms. Like *Your Hit Parade*, both shows were networked

by CBS. If you hear them now, these programmes reveal Sinatra's marvellous consistency in performance. And Sinatra just got better and better on *Songs By Sinatra* (CBS, sponsored by Old Gold Cigarettes), which began in the fall of 1945 and continued until the end of 1947.

Sinatra's last major radio series of the Forties (ending in the spring of 1950) was *Light-Up Time* (sponsored again by Lucky Strike and networked by NBC). Although there was much to commend about his singing for most of the series' duration, there is no doubt that Sinatra's troubled times were starting to make inroads on The Voice itself during the last six months of the series.

Duets didn't start in the Nineties – of course not. Frank, on radio, with Dinah Shore.

GIGS

The reviews of Sinatra's earliest solo gigs all gave praise – some grudgingly – to the singer's night-club performances and his rarer appearances in concert. Even the Doubting Thomases were surprised not just at how well he sang, but also at the way he came across on-stage. His deportment impressed the most hard-bitten critics; his timing and the way he used the stage (like other vocalists, he was more or less restricted to centre-stage due to the limitations imposed by stand-up microphones in use during the Forties) soon had audiences eating out of his hand.

Just how well Sinatra performed live can be gleaned from the faded cuttings of magazine and newspaper reviews: reactions tended to be ecstatic. And if perhaps you chance to meet up with someone who actually attended a gig some 50 years ago, they'll almost certainly confirm that Sinatra was unforgettable.

Writing for a special "Sinatra-Is-Back" *Billboard* supplement in 1973, noted jazz critic/author, Leonard Feather, remembered the first time he experienced one of Sinatra's solo performances. It was at the historic Riobamba Club engagement in 1943. Recalled the British-born Feather, "The smart, sophisticated night club crowd fixed its attention on the skinny youth as he approached the microphone. I sat at a not-far-from-the ringside table, watching him weave his head around in a gentle persuasive manner as he sang 'Embraceable You' and 'As Time Goes By'. It didn't take too much receptivity to notice particularly the combined effect of voice, delivery and personality on the feminine segment of the audience."

For a serious-minded performer such as Sinatra, reviews from critics such as Feather, George T Simon, and Dave Dexter Jr were more important than all the high-profile write-ups in the *New York Times* or the *Washington Post* put together. A good crit in either *Down Beat* or *Metronome* – publications for music *aficionados*, particularly lovers of jazz and swing – was eminently more satisfying to musicians and singers, especially since it would be read by their peers. Even though Sinatra seems always to have resented reviews that were not in the affirmative, music papers at least were more likely to provide a fair-minded representation of the way performers and bands played.

To assess at first hand just how excellent Sinatra actually sounded in live performance was almost impossible until recently. Just how superbly he could (and did) sing has now been demonstrated on one CD release at least, *The Unheard Frank Sinatra/Radio Rarities 1943-1949, Volume 3*, which appeared a couple of years ago. There are two extremely important examples of live Frank Sinatra on this

The Forties Frank – year-by-year he was becoming a star performer – records, movies, concerts, on radio . . .

recording, both from Hollywood Bowl concerts, dated August 1945 and August 1948, respectively.

The first comprises a five-song contribution Sinatra made to a special Academy Night Concert given in tribute to an ailing Jerome Kern. With Stordahl conducting his own arrangements and accompanied by a local symphony orchestra, Sinatra's quality of performance was astonishing. Starting with a wistful, beautifully-paced version of Kern's then popular "Long Ago And Far Away", he went on to sing a warm, gentle version of "I Should Care" (which he'd recorded for Columbia, five months before) and a deftly-phrased "What Makes The Sunset?" (from his then current movie, *Anchors Aweigh!*).

Sinatra followed these up with an absolutely stunning interpretation of "If I Loved You" from the smash-hit Broadway production of *Carousel*. Of all the many versions – on record as well as live – he would perform over the years ahead, the Hollywood Bowl/1945 performance is the finest. Indeed, it is almost certainly the finest by any vocalist at any time.

To conclude his segment, Sinatra invested "Ol' Man River" with real authority and conviction. Like the previous number, this performance contained everything that made the singer a legend in his lifetime: the control is breathtaking, the diction and phrasing immaculate and deep feeling suffuses the entire reading. As you can hear today, the deep spell the singer wove was nearly broken a couple of times when some bobbysoxer squealed from the audience – but never quite; Sinatra quietly remonstrated with his young fans, in a firm, friendly and avuncular manner ...

His appearance at the same venue three years later was, once again, top-class Sinatra. Not quite as extraordinary, maybe, as 1945, but consistently brilliant nonetheless. This time the occasion was a Music For The Wounded charity.

Second time around, the programme was shorter. "Time After Time" had already passed into pop-music lore as Sinatra's personal property – and this was as fine a version as most others. "The Girl That I Marry" was similar to the Columbia recording of 1946 – full of charm, with the pauses-and-hesitations part of his technique quietly brought to bear. The finale was similar to 1945, except that on this occasion Sinatra chose the complete "Soliloquy" from *Carousel*. It was a stunning performance, which deftly removed – somehow – the basic schmaltz from this overblown opus and turned it into something else.

These days, serious Sinatra admirers are still patiently awaiting further fascinating insights into the live Sinatra of the Forties. In all probability, though, there aren't likely to be too many additions to the catalogue. After all, mobile tape-recordists were few-and-far-between in those days.

Oh that someone like the legendary Jerry Newman, who documented so much jazz magic of the Thirties, Forties and Fifties, had been prepared to lug his machine to at least one Sinatra gig in the post-Dorsey years ... !

Now hear this! Frank gives Judy Garland and her husband Sid Luft the gospel truth.

TELEVISION

TV was still in its infancy at the end of the Forties. Sinatra's own first involvement started on May 27, 1950, as guest on *Star Spangled Review* (NBC). By October, he had been accorded his first regular series – *The Frank Sinatra Show* – which went out between October 1950 and June 1951. It was sponsored by Bulova and broadcast by CBS. Episodes were mostly an hour in duration, although some lasted 45 minutes. A follow-up series, this one sponsored by Echo, ran from October 1951 to April 1952. Regulars on both series were the ever-faithful Axel Stordahl plus wife, and singer June Hutton, together with her vocal group, the Hutton Tones.

The series projected Frank Sinatra's talents in a pretty dull way visually. Viewed in retrospect, the settings and backdrops were of amateur-hour standard, the scripts not only dated but naive. Sinatra himself was sometimes clad in casual gear – check shirt and slacks, for example – in an apparent effort to present him in a more laid-back, accessible manner.

Perhaps because of professional and personal problems – especially an alarming throat-haemorrhage incident at the Copacabana – Sinatra's singing tended to vary. This could have been evidence of the strain from years of virtual non-stop performing.

However, there were occasions when any technical shortcomings were compensated for by a new, more basic kind of emotional delivery, for example on "You Are Love". And there were also intimations of a would-be swinger on "Get Happy". But for Frank Sinatra, full acceptance as a TV personality would have to wait until the latter half of the Fifties ...

The Decline & Despair

The decline in the fortunes of Frank Sinatra during the late Forties and early Fifties was as dramatic as it was comprehensive. Failure touched nearly every area of his life.

Only Sinatra's most loyal fans stood by him as his professional reputation waned – slowly, at first, then accelerating at an alarming pace. Even the birth of his third child – Christine, in June 1948 – failed to lift the gathering gloom and wife Nancy was soon to file for separate maintenance.

Though he rarely sang poorly, the quality of Sinatra's early movies provided little scope for his acting ambitions: it hardly came as a shock when, at his own request, he was freed from his contract with MGM in April 1950.

Sinatra wasn't about to make a big comeback on TV either. A five-year CBS contract, guaranteeing him $250,000 a year, ended prematurely. Right from the opening broadcast on October 7, 1950, critics gave *The Frank Sinatra Show* a collective thumbs-down. A second series, premiered on October 9, 1951, foreclosed the following April, costing CBS a rumoured $1 million.

By September 1952, Sinatra had ended his 10-year association with Columbia Records still owing the company a reported $110,000 in unearned advances.

In December, the William Morris Agency took over from MCA as Sinatra's management company. MCA claimed he owed them $40,000 in back commissions – Sinatra said it was only $26,000. Just to rub salt into the gaping financial wound, the Internal Revenue presented the singer with a claim for $109,996 in back taxes.

On the gigs front, things were a little brighter. Sinatra may not have been pulling in the crowds like he used to but the applause – from critics and audiences alike – was still warm and genuine.

On one occasion, however, Sinatra experienced the ultimate singer's nightmare. At New York's Copacabana in March 1950, he was suffering from a throat ailment. Against doctor's advice, he came out for his third show in one evening. Suddenly, in mid-song, no sound came from his mouth. For several seconds, he was rooted to the spot looking terrified, then fled for the safety of his dressing room. Sinatra had suffered a sub-mucosal throat haemorrhage and this time acceded to his physician's request not to try to sing – or even talk – for at least two weeks.

Around this time, the Hit Parade was dominated by other male vocalists such as Johnny Ray, Guy Mitchell and Frankie Laine. Sinatra was also being outsold by the likes of Billy Eckstine, Perry Como and Nat King Cole. Between 1950 and 1952, he managed a trifling four Top 10 entries.

On top of all this, there was Ava Gardner, the voluptuous movie star from Grabtown, North Carolina, with whom Sinatra was totally infatuated: their doomed relationship had begun in the mid-Forties.

Ava Lavinia Gardner became the second Mrs Frank Sinatra in November 1951, a year after Nancy had secured an interlocutory decree of divorce.

Sinatra's courtship of Ava, and his attempts to keep their marriage intact, took a huge toll, physically, mentally and psychologically. Numerous close friends have said that, despite the all-too-frequent public rows and brawling, theirs was a genuine love affair ... although Ava's love, say many, turned to something approaching hatred.

The combination of a fast-fading career and troubled love life led Sinatra to despair, even, it has been alleged, to attempted suicide through drug overdose on August 31, 1951. Sinatra said it was just an allergic reaction to a small dose of sleeping tablets. Many years later, his long-time valet, George Jacobs, was sure his boss *did* try to take his life: it was only because he returned in the nick of time, that the singer survived ...

As 1951 ended, omens for the future looked bleak – if indeed there was to be a future. Very bleak indeed.

Two in love – wedding-day bliss for Ava and Frank. But their happiness was not destined to last.

The Golden Years

WHEN Sinatra finished reading James Jones' best-selling novel, *From Here To Eternity*, he was certain of one thing. He knew he was made for the part of the gutsy, ill-fated GI, Angelo Maggio, in the forthcoming movie from Columbia Pictures.

Sinatra: "Maggio for a grand" . . . Cohn: "Your're a *singer*!"

The story of military life set in Schofield Barracks, Honolulu, around the time of Pearl Harbor, *From Here To Eternity* was full of dramatic action and ready-made for cinema. Motivated as much by the book's impressive early sales figures as by unanimous praise from the critics, Columbia Pictures' infamous studio chief, Harry Cohn, astutely snapped up the screen rights, decreeing that no expense be spared on this production and that only the biggest stars would do.

This was 1952 and Sinatra's career was on the skids: record sales were down; he owed thousands in back taxes to the IRS; his record label was dropping him; his agency was dropping him; his television and radio shows were dropping him. Things got so bad, Sinatra even started being nice to members of the press. Unfortunately, sections of the press didn't always reciprocate.

Looking for a lifeline, Sinatra came to believe that his own and Maggio's fates were intertwined – only the role of this fictitious Italian-American could save him from the vicious circle of gloom and despair. Since reading the novel, he had closely identified with the character,

"I knew Maggio. I went to school with him in Hoboken. I was beaten-up with him. I might have been Maggio ..."

But Sinatra was up against intense competition for the part. The problem was that it called for a "heavyweight" performance and Sinatra was viewed as a lightweight: he was a "singer not an actor".

Forgetting the demands of his constant on-off relationship with second wife, screen beauty Ava Gardner, Sinatra knew he had to act speedily. Buddy Adler, who produced *From Here To Eternity*, remembered later just how persistent Sinatra became, once casting had been announced. He started badgering Adler for the part of Maggio and wouldn't let it drop.

Though not unsympathetic, Adler reminded Sinatra he was looking for a "serious" actor. As time passed, Sinatra's hopes began to fade. In desperation, he urged Ava, the influential movie star, to intercede on his behalf with the ruthless Cohn. She did. No dice. As a final resort, Sinatra called Cohn personally. The reaction was predictable: not a chance. With just a trace of sadism, Cohn, again, reminded his caller that portraying Maggio was a task for a real actor – an actor of experience and proven ability – ... "and you're a *singer*".

Despite Sinatra's entreaties, Cohn remained immovable. Finally, Frank tossed in his last card: he would play Maggio for the give-away price of $1000 a week. At last, Cohn hesitated. But there was no promise of even a screen-test. Sinatra would have to sweat it out until other applicants – of proven acting ability – had had their chance.

Finally, the list of possible candidates was down to three: Eli Wallach, with no previous experience in films but a stage actor since 1940, was the favourite – and Cohn's own choice; Harvey Lembeck, a comedian and character actor, who had been in movies less than two years; and Frank Sinatra, singer supreme, who, at the last ditch, had received the call from Buddy Adler after he'd almost given up hope.

After the three had screen-tested, it became clear that Sinatra had impressed Adler, director Fred Zinnemann, screenplay author Don Taradash ... and even the reluctant Harry Cohn! Cohn brought in his wife, Joan Cohn, whose opinion he valued, to make a judgement. She agreed with the others that Wallach's Maggio had been brilliant – the best of the three.

"... Working with Burt Lancaster and, above all, Montgomery Clift [was] a challenge and an inspiration."

But, said Mrs Cohn, he was too muscular, didn't look like an Italian; both of which points counted in skinny Sinatra's favour. Nevertheless, Wallach remained her husband's choice.

Sinatra soon got wind of Cohn's preference. Forlorn, he left with Ava for Nairobi, where she was due to start shooting on her latest MGM picture, *Mogambo*, alongside Grace Kelly, Clark Gable and Donald Sinden. At this point, Gardner had problems of her own – with tough, hard-talking director, John Ford, for one, not to mention the frequent, often public, rows with her husband.

Less than a week after the couple arrived in Africa, in January 1953, Sinatra's torture ended. A cable from Adler announced that the part of Maggio was his and that he would receive a fee of $8000.

It turned out that Sinatra had been given the part, not exclusively on account of his compelling screen-test, but because Eli Wallach had pulled out to star in Tennessee Williams' new play, *El Camino*. Other factors included Wallach's refusal to sign the seven-year contract Cohn demanded and, perhaps more importantly, his insistence on getting double the salary Columbia were prepared to pay.

Even though he knew his marriage was balanced on a knife-edge, Sinatra left Ava in Africa to join the rest of the *Eternity* cast. Shooting commenced in Hollywood at the beginning of March 1953, then moved on location to Hawaii. The six weeks required to complete the movie were an education for Sinatra. Working with top pros such as Burt Lancaster, Deborah Kerr, Donna Reed, Jack Warden and, above all, Montgomery Clift, proved both a challenge and an inspiration.

On the set of *From Here To Eternity*, Sinatra and Clift became close friends. Sinatra happily confessed,

"I learned more about acting from him than I ever knew before."

Sinatra's metamorphosis into an actor of true worth owed much to the influence of Clift (arguably, the most sensitive male actor in movie history) and the total commitment he brought to the central role of Private Robert E Lee Prewitt. You can see Sinatra's debt to the short-lived Clift in *Eternity* itself, as well as in many of Sinatra's acting assignments during the Fifties and Sixties. The hunched shoulders, the sometimes clenched fists and the haunted look – they were all physical trademarks inherited from Monty Clift by Sinatra, who used them, intelligently and naturally, to his own advantage.

The film's rushes astounded even those at Columbia who had firmly believed *From Here To Eternity* was a sure-fire winner from the outset. On its release, the critics gushed praise and cinema-goers throughout the States flocked in droves to see it – many returned for a second, or even a third, sitting ensuring that the movie grossed in excess of $19 million first time around.

The production duly accrued 13 nominations for Academy Awards, a figure equalled by *Gone With The Wind* (1939) and bettered previously only by *All About Eve* in 1950 (14). *From Here To Eternity* became one of the hottest favourites in years for Best Picture and duly received that highest-prized Oscar. Individual Oscars went to Lancaster, Clift, Reed and Sinatra himself.

At the Awards Ceremony, on March 25, 1954, Sinatra was accompanied by his daughter Nancy and son Frank Jr. When presenter Mercedes McCambridge called out his name as winner, there was an instant roar from the assembled motion picture luminaries – an ovation that exceeded all others that night. Sinatra had proved his point: as well as supreme singer, he was now acknowledged as an outstanding actor.

An ecstatic Sinatra stepped athletically up to the podium to receive his trophy. A brief, staccato acceptance speech included the words, "If I start thanking everybody, I'll do a one-reeler!"

In more subdued mood later at a post-ceremony party, he telephoned Dolly Sinatra, his mother. As Arnold Shaw

(in *Sinatra: Retreat Of The Romantic*) recalled 15 years later, "Friends who could not help overhearing the end of the conversation report that it consisted largely of phrases like 'Yes, mama' and 'No, mama'. A few minutes earlier, he had been the great showman who had twice taken the entertainment world by storm. Now he was suddenly a lonely, love-hungry, small boy seeking his mother's affection and approval by parading his fantastic accomplishment before her."

Sinatra and Donna Reed receive their Eternity Oscars.

The Oscar Award was the most eye-catching moment yet in what some commentators were beginning to call an amazing comeback. Far away from the brouhaha surrounding *From Here To Eternity*, arrangements had already been made to ensure that Sinatra The Singer would once again hit the high notes.

When Sinatra's ten-year contract with Columbia Records expired at the end of 1952, reaction from other companies, including the minor ones, was distinctly underwhelming, even when the William Morris office (Sinatra's new management/publicity agency) applied considerable diplomatic pressure.

Early in 1953, Capitol Records, the leading independent company, came up with an offer. It was in stark contrast to Columbia's generous proposition way back in the heady days of 1943: there were to be no advance payments and, in addition, the new signing had to bear all costs relating to musicians, as well as any fees incurred for arrangements and music-copying.

Whatever his private thoughts on the deal, Frank Sinatra had little option but to accept – that was, if he wanted to resume a full-time recording career. So, accept he did. The only time Sinatra balked at plans for his future outlined by Alan W Livingston, the label's A&R chief, was over the choice of Dave Dexter Jr as his personal producer. Before taking up a career in the record industry, Dexter had been a respected jazz and pop critic on publications such as *Down Beat, Metronome* and *Billboard*. As Dexter remembered years later in his absorbing autobiography, *Replay*, Sinatra's reaction was explosive,

***In The Wee Small Hours** – a collection of superior ballads about lost or unrequited love and loneliness.*

"That bastard? I won't work with him. He's the jerk who rapped my records in Down Beat. Screw 'im, who needs 'im?"

When Livingston passed on Sinatra's comments, Dexter agreed that, in among numerous good reviews over the years, some had been less than complimentary – as a critic who took his job seriously, he had to tell the truth when things were bad. Quite obviously, Sinatra had never forgotten any of the less-than-euphoric notices ... and nor was he inclined to forgive them.

At first, Dexter was incensed by Sinatra's rejection. But, then, he saw how ironic the situation was. As he told Livingston, "Here's a guy who is dead on his ass. He's been deserted by all but a few of his friends, he's without a job, and he's brushed off every day by the record companies, the picture studios, and the radio and television networks. But I believe in his basic talent … and I'm the only guy in the world who's willing to risk my job in spending $100,000 or more of my company's money trying to bring the sonofabitch back – and he fluffs me. Next time you talk to him, Alan, tell him to shove it. The feeling is mutual."

The fact that Dave Dexter genuinely did believe in Sinatra's talent is borne out by his comments elsewhere in his book. In his own words,

> ## *"Ingrate or not, there's only one Francis Albert Sinatra and in 987 years there will never be another quite like him."*

In the end, Dexter *did* get the chance to record with his rejecter, even if it was for one occasion only – and for Capitol Records too. This was at a session on December 13, 1954, which produced two numbers – "Melody Of Love" and "I'm Gonna Live Till I Die" – and was to be Sinatra's one-and-only recording with Ray Anthony fronting the orchestra.

Prepared for the worst, but intent on doing a professional job as temporary replacement for Voyle Gilmore, the regular A&R man, Dexter had no trouble with Sinatra. At first meeting, Sinatra stretched out a hand and said, softly, "Nice to see you". During the mastering of the two takes, there were no problems. Both men did their jobs in predictably first-class fashion. And Sinatra's brief farewell comment was cheerful, not at all unfriendly …

In fact, right from the very earliest Capitol sessions in 1953,

Sinatra's incredible renaissance was apparent on record. Old buddy Axel Stordahl was responsible for three of the four arrangements – former Dorsey associate Heine Beau scored "Lean Baby" in the style of composer Billy May – but only two of the four titles were issued at the time, comprising Sinatra's debut 78 rpm release. British songwriter Billy Reid's "I'm Walking Behind You" provided Sinatra with a satisfying return to the charts. Spending 10 weeks in the US Hit Parade, the single rose as high as seventh place.

It was to take almost a year before a Sinatra record gained a foothold inside the US Top 10 again. This came with the title song of the movie "Young At Heart", which stayed 22 weeks in the charts and got to Number 2. Later in 1954, another film song, "Three Coins In The Fountain", gave him a further smash-hit single, with a place inside the US Top 5. In Britain, though, it was even more successful, going to Number 1.

After the "dark days", these successes were immensely encouraging for Sinatra and his followers – including, of course, Capitol – and his re-emergence as a world-wide singing star went hand in hand with new technology. Sinatra's arrival at Capitol coincided with the development of micro-groove recordings in general and the long-play record in particular. Sinatra rapidly became the leading light in the LP field, not only as a consistent best-seller, but for the consistently superb quality of his performances.

From his very first long-playing release, Frank Sinatra's reputation in the album field was established. In terms of sheer all-round quality, *Songs For Young Lovers* remains a milestone in the history of recorded music. So, too, was its concept of "mood" – and the way Sinatra and his musical director introduced and sustained that mood throughout.

It is significant, too, that the name of arranger/conductor Nelson Riddle was prominent, together with that of Sinatra, on the sleeve of that first LP (even though it would take many years for the connoisseur to discover that the rhythm items such as "They Can't Take That Away From Me" and "I Get a Kick Out Of You" were actually arranged by a past Sinatra associate, George Siravo).

Nelson Riddle (1921-1985) was born in Oradell, New Jersey. His early career found him playing in the trombone sections of the swing bands of Charlie Spivak, Jerry Wald and Tommy Dorsey. It

Sinatra and Doris Day co-star in the ever-green *Young At Heart*.

Nelson Riddle – "Best writer for Sinatra".

was during this period of his musical development (1940-1945) that he first learned about arranging. After Dorsey, there came a stint with a US army band; then, on demobilization, Riddle played with the Bob Crosby Orchestra and, briefly, with Dorsey once again. Riddle's enviable reputation as one of pop music's greatest arrangers reached its zenith during the Fifties when he collaborated with Sinatra for Capitol. Theirs was a unique blending of two distinctive talents and it came to be rated at least the equal of the earlier Sinatra-Stordahl partnership.

Certainly, Stordahl and Riddle were the most important of all Sinatra's music-director associates; if Riddle qualifies as the best writer to work with the singer, that was down to his ability to create superbly-crafted scores in both ballad and rhythmic settings – whereas Stordahl's reputation rests exclusively in the former area.

Both men benefited from their close association with Sinatra in as far as it enabled them to make their mark in the motion-picture industry. Here, though, their achievements differed. Whereas Stordahl's film work involved only Sinatra movies, Riddle went on to become a Hollywood regular in his own right. Indeed, he not only won an Oscar for Best Scoring: Original Song Score And/Or Adaptation for *The Great Gatsby* (1974), but also received Academy nominations for four other movies.

Even though Riddle's writing helped enhance Sinatra's appearances on television and in movies, it is mostly remembered for the numerous collaborations on record. During the Fifties, Sinatra recordings would benefit from the written backgrounds provided by a select few arrangers – Billy May and Gordon Jenkins were two others, whose services were used on several occasions – but inevitably it was Nelson Riddle's name which cropped up on by far the majority of Sinatra's Capitol recordings – whether rotating at speeds of 78 rpm (for the first five years), 45 rpm or 33 1/3 rpm.

After the rebirth of Sinatra the Actor, Sinatra the Singer also had to change to keep up with the times – and now he had acquired an ability to swing with real conviction, in a manner that hitherto he'd only hinted at.

Sinatra seemed to live inside the record studios in the Fifties.

Songs For Young Lovers, a satisfying mix of supreme balladeering and relaxed, jazz-based rhythmic singing, set the tone for a near-decade of mostly superlative recording projects. That timeless classic's successor, *Swing Easy*, drew fresh strength from the new-found rhythmic pulse. Recorded at two consecutive dates in April 1954, it also contains some of Riddle's finest rhythmic scores and Sinatra responded in full measure, to produce eight first-class performances, which together authenticate the album's title.

The addition of Sinatra's new "swinging" style to sensitively handled ballads appealed widely, not only to those who bought his records and went to see his movies but also to a handsome (and growing) number of fellow vocalists, songwriters, composers, arrangers and instrumentalists.

The genuine affection in which Sinatra was held during the Fifties by so many diverse jazz musicians and singers indicated his affinity with and respect for many different styles of music.

This was borne out by a special "Musicians' Musician" Poll conducted by author/critic, Leonard Feather, for inclusion in his *Encyclopaedia Yearbook Of Jazz* (1956). Sinatra won the Male Singer category hands down, polling 56 votes to runners-up Nat Cole's 13 and Billy Eckstine's 11. (Louis Armstrong and Bing Crosby were among the also-rans.)

Not only were Fifties jazz musicians hip to the post-*Eternity* Sinatra but jazz fans responded to his music with an enthusiasm that brought back memories of his amazing popularity in the Forties before he'd left the Dorsey band. For instance, readers of the influential *Down Beat* magazine, who had transferred their allegiance during the years of decline to rival Billy Eckstine, between 1948 and 1952, and to Nat Cole in 1953, restored the name of Sinatra to poll-topping status in 1954. Readers of rival publication *Metronome* likewise voted him Singer of the Year. And leading trade paper, *Billboard*, through its annual poll of disc jockeys, bestowed a triple honour upon Sinatra – Top Male Vocalist, with "Young At Heart" and *Swing Easy* adjudged Best Record of the Year and Best LP of the Year, respectively.

The busy-busy year of 1955 was dominated by film-making and

regular visits to Capitol Tower. Yet there was still time for Sinatra, accompanied by daughter Nancy, to fly to Australia during the summer to undertake a 12-day tour during which he played four concerts. The Aussies accorded him a tremendous reception at each of the gigs – his debut performances in the country – for which he earned fees in excess of $40,000.

Sinatra's hits during 1955 included "Learnin' The Blues" (which topped the US Hit Parade and peaked at Number 2 in Britain), "Love And Marriage" (US Number 5; Number 3 in UK), and the movie theme "(Love Is) The Tender Trap" (Number 7 in the US; Number 2 in the UK). Surprisingly, "You, My Love" from *Young At Heart* never quite made it as a Top 10 entry in either territory.

Certainly, though, the single most important recording event of 1955 was the completion of *In The Wee Small Hours*, a collection of superior ballads about lost or unrequited love and loneliness, which was immediately acknowledged as a masterpiece. Throughout the succeeding decades, the album has retained a magic and potency that ensure its status for posterity. Backing up Sinatra's peerless interpretation on such classics as "Last Night When We Were Young", "I Get Along Without You Very Well" and "It Never Entered My Mind" are some of Nelson Riddle's most masterful scores. Indeed, for many connoisseurs, *In The Wee Small Hours* has no peer.

Of all Sinatra's recordings of the Fifties, none was more widely-loved than *Songs For Swingin' Lovers* (1956). With Riddle once again the guiding light, Sinatra's performances throughout a generous 16-track presentation are buoyant and uplifting.

If you had to pick out one track from this collection of gems, it would have to be the electrifying "I've Got You Under My Skin", complete with its blast-furnace four-bar trombone solo by Milt Bernhardt. *Swingin' Lovers* was a global success but nowhere was it more popular than in the UK. It actually entered the *New Musical Express* singles charts in mid-1956 and succeeded in reaching Number 12, an absolutely unrepeatable feat.

An archetypal Sinatra shot from Capitol Tower during the Fifties. The ever-present fedora matched the swingin' image – but the music lingers longest.

The other side of the coin, in commercial if not artistic terms, came sadly in the form of another Sinatra album from Capitol. In its own way, *Close To You* (1957) is supremely representative of Frank Sinatra, the *Meistersinger*, much like *Wee Small Hours*, *Only The Lonely*, *Swingin' Lovers* or any of the other top-quality sets.

The album contains a close-miked, intimate singing that is as exquisite as anything Sinatra would commit to vinyl at any stage of his career. There's not a "merely average" performance on any track. Yet, having been issued, deleted, reissued, then deleted again more frequently than practically any of its companion-pieces, *Close To You* probably remains one of Sinatra's poorest-selling Capitol LPs. (Only on a first release in the US did it achieve anything like the kind of sales it deserved, reaching the Top 5 in the *Billboard* album charts.)

If any one other Sinatra LP can be considered a direct rival to *In The Wee Small Hours*, then it would have to be another Sinatra-Riddle collaboration in similar mood and setting: *Only The Lonely*, taped over three years later, finds the singer performing with even greater depth and emotional conviction. It also has Riddle's greatest collection of arrangements under one roof – certainly, his work rarely if ever sounded as emotionally-involving anywhere else.

Here again, the song selection is practically beyond reproach and includes what is probably *the* quintessential series of Sinatra performances ... *Only The Lonely* became a Top LP in the States and remained in *Billboard*'s album charts for an amazing 120 weeks. It also earned a Grammy Award – this time not for the singer, the arranger/conductor or the producer Dave Cavanaugh (his first session with Sinatra) but instead, the accolade was awarded for Best Album Cover. Still, it did become the Number 2 best-selling album of 1958.

The top-selling LP of the year was also Sinatra's. *Come Fly With Me*, with its mixture of moods and *tempi* as well as its around-the-world theme, was the first time that former Barnet and Miller trumpeter/arranger Billy May had worked with Sinatra, except for some uncredited charts relating to broadcast dates in the Forties. *Come Fly With Me* was one of May's earliest opportunities to write for strings and woodwinds in addition to his more customary big-band-swing commissions. Following the world-wide success of *Come Fly With Me*, he was reunited with Sinatra for two further Capitol albums, as well as for singles sessions inevitably focused on the rhythmic side of Sinatra's output.

Gordon Jenkins (1910-1984) was the oldest of Sinatra's three

main arrangers. He handled the ballad dates not undertaken by Riddle, providing highly-emotional writing for strings/woodwinds, often classicically styled after the fashion of Rachmaninoff or Tchaikovsky. After a 10-year association with the American Decca company, he joined Capitol's artists roster as staff arranger. His *Manhattan Tower* suite, recorded in 1956, became something of a benchmark in the field of light music composition.

The first collaboration between Jenkins and Sinatra resulted in the album, *Where Are You?* (1957). Although well-received by critics, its reputation as another masterpiece has only been widely subscribed to in the past 20 years. Sinatra later described working with Jenkins' arrangements as "like being back in the womb". Certainly, emotions are to the fore on this album – although never cloyingly so - and that's down to both leading participants' input.

Their next studio get-together came just a few months after the completion of *Where Are You?* Less important undoubtedly than its predecessor, *A Jolly Christmas* has nonetheless long since been recognized as probably the finest of its festive type. And *No One Cares*, Sinatra and Jenkins' final collaboration, completed two years later, was even more doom-laden than *Where Are You?* – deeply moving but never quite its equal.

By the time *No One Cares* was released, Sinatra's contribution to the history of recorded popular vocal music was unrivalled. And there were plenty more hit singles to come, including "All The Way", the Oscar-winning Cahn-Van Heusen opus composed for *The Joker Is Wild*, which got near the top of the charts both in Britain and the States. Another Sinatra movie, *A Hole In The Head* (1960), yielded further large-scale British success with the semi-novelty, "High Hopes". It also provided the creators of "All The Way" with a second Oscar statuette for Best Song.

By now, the Capitol label was associated with a line of immensely popular movie musicals. The best-loved of these remains *High Society* (1956), with Sinatra appearing alongside his mentor, Bing Crosby, on the first of only two occasions. There was also an unforgettable appearance by Louis Armstrong, in an acting-singing-playing role with his band, the All Stars. *Pal Joey* (1957) was pure Sinatra, with individual vocal features – both dubbed – for co-stars Rita Hayworth and Kim Novak restricted to one apiece. *Can-Can* (1960) was something of a disappointment, yet contained one stunning performance that ranks, together with "The Lady Is A Tramp" from *Pal Joey*, as his finest on-screen singing. this was a slower-than-usual reading of Cole Porter's "It's All Right With Me" that could scarcely have been improved upon.

Towards the end of the Fifties, the relationship between Capitol Records and their most in-demand artist changed. Sinatra had achieved more or less everything he wanted and in the way he wanted – let it not be forgotten that he was also unofficial co-producer at all his sessions – and he could not have been too unhappy with the results of his sessions since early 1953.

But Sinatra had gradually become convinced that it was time to cut the link with Capitol and start his own record company. By 1959, he had obtained a deal which enabled him to own the masters he cut through Essex Productions, one of his own companies, which in turn were assigned to Capitol for processing and distribution.

Sinatra conducts, not sings, and with not a little skill – something which Gordon Jenkins (inset, with Garland) did full-time and consummately well.

Unsurprisingly, when he asked Capitol to release him the same year, they were simply not interested. For openers, the contract which bound the two parties together was not due to expire until November 1962 and Sinatra was of course still a red-hot property in the record business, as everywhere else in the show business firmament.

True to form, Sinatra was furious and made it plain to his employers how he felt. Sadly, there were a few occasions when his unhappiness with Capitol seemed to spill over into his final recordings for the company.

One result was a casual – *too* casual by far – approach to much of his swing-singing on the May-arranged *Come Swing With Me* (1961). The title track for 1960's *Nice 'N' Easy* – a substantial hit, in single format – was easily the best part of that album. The rest comprises re-workings of a batch of Columbia favourites; no more than two selections, at most, are improvements.

Worst of all was a slapdash LP, *Sinatra's Swingin' Session* (like *Nice 'N' Easy*, masterminded by Riddle). Taken as a whole, the overall contents represent the only real glitch in the entire Sinatra Capitol discography. And the reason why many individual tracks are so brief was down to Riddle being asked to up most, if not all, the tempos. What at first appeared to be an apocryphal story was confirmed to the author by the arranger/conductor himself many years later. Even today, the idea of such a situation arising seems, at the least, unlikely: after all, didn't we all believe, for sure, that Sinatra was the total perfectionist inside a recording studio … ?

Musically, Sinatra had usually managed to record the kind of material he liked. Of course, Capitol supplied him with new songs at regular intervals, which, hopefully, would turn into single-play releases … and then hits. "Hey! Jealous Lover", recorded in April 1956, became a major US hit later in the year. The fact that Sinatra was not at all fond of the number was confirmed the following year, when he performed it at a concert at Seattle's Civic Auditorium. Over Riddle's intro, he told his audience, "I absolutely and unequivocally detest this song." "Hey! Jealous Lover" was the kind of new number with which Capitol hoped to sell Sinatra to the youthful, ever-expanding rock'n'roll market – being an awkward amalgam of his kind of music and the beat sounds prevalent at the time, it failed to be a hit.

Whatever Sinatra's feelings toward this particular item in his discography, they can surely have been no more cynical than his reactions to an earlier session, held in March 1955, at which he recorded two other pseudo-rock items – his first attempts to enter this area of mid-Fifties pop music. Both "Two Hearts, Two Kisses" and "From The Bottom To The Top" were doomed to obscurity in double-quick time. It may have been a brave attempt on the part of Capitol in general, and producer Dave Cavanaugh in particular, to move their major star on to pastures new. Cavanaugh – parading under the pseudonym of "Big Dave" – arranged for an accompanying band, plus a vocal group calling itself the Nuggets, and played some mean rootin'-tootin' tenor-sax. Predictably, neither track took off … principally, because Sinatra could not – and would not – rock'n'roll …

In 1957, Frank Sinatra made one of his occasional verbal outbursts against the new pop music of the day. No punches were pulled, either. Quoth he (on rock'n'roll),

Sinatra and distinguished, specially invited studio guests listen intently to a playback.

"It fosters almost totally negative and destructive reactions in young people. My only deep sorrow is the unrelenting insistence of recording and motion-picture companies upon purveying this most brutal, degenerate, vicious form of expression."

(Sinatra's reactionary opinion of modern pop was to soften considerably during the following decade – thanks largely to daughter Nancy's success as a recording artist. This culminated in a massive Number 1 disc in 1966 – "These Boots Are Made For Walking" – and, the following year, another chart-topping triumph ... this time in duet with her dad on "Somethin' Stupid"....)

Along with many regular visits to Capitol's recording studios during the Fifties, Sinatra made numerous appearances on radio (culminating in the series *To Be Perfectly Frank*, containing his finest singing ever on the airwaves). Mid-1954 was also the start of an extraordinary increase in movie-making activity which meant that, during 1955, Sinatra was involved in no fewer than five major film productions. Towards the end of the decade, though, Sinatra's involvement with radio had all but ceased and it was during this period that he resumed his attempts to establish a reputation as a

Sinatra opens the new Ziegfeld Follies Winter Garden, NYC, in 1955. Gladys Gardner (far left) appeared in the 1915 edition of the original show, at age 15.

major TV artist. The first series of *The Frank Sinatra Show* was transmitted in 1957.

Because of his increasing commitments to films and recording, Sinatra's availability for live performances became much more limited than his many admirers would have wished. Indeed, the majority might well have had to wait for years to see him on-stage, unless they could afford to visit Las Vegas for his appearances first at Caesar's Palace and then at the Sands Hotel.

Frank's first gigs at the Sands took place during the latter period of the "comeback" years. He was to play regular seasons there for the next 13 years. From the beginning, after obtaining the necessary gambling licence from the local Nevada state authority, he had invested $54,000 of his own money in the huge entertainment palace. Whether or not you could say that either the Sands Hotel or Caesar's Palace represent the Mecca of artistic inspiration, nevertheless, for the next three decades and more, these kind of venues were to become mainstays for Sinatra's live appearances.

After the frenzied activity of the early Fifties, punters might have thought that the rest of the decade might find Sinatra easing off a bit, at least in his private life. No chance of that.

In July 1957, the divorce decree Ava Gardner had long sought was finally issued. In the same year, *Jazz* magazine chose Sinatra and Billie Holiday as joint Singers of the Year; Walter Winchell (*American Weekly*) called him the All-Round Entertainer of the Year; meanwhile *Metronome*'s Bill Coss said Sinatra was "the most complete, the most fantastic symbol of American maleness yet discovered".

Among the sad events of the latter half of the Fifties were the deaths of Sinatra's hero-buddy Bogart (1957, from throat cancer) and Manie Sachs (1958, heart attack). The death of

Tommy Dorsey, 51, was something which must have brought Sinatra's memories of the big-band days flooding back, temporarily, at least. The veteran bandleader had choked to death in his sleep on the night of November 26, 1956. Sadly, no one can recall messages of condolence from Sinatra. It would seem he had never forgiven Dorsey for giving him such a hard time when he left the band to embark on his solo career.

As the years went by, Sinatra's record- and movie-making continued unabated; TV involvement picked up; and there was still time for regular live performances. There were to be further hit singles to complement increasingly successful albums – although nothing as classy as "All The Way", or the irresistible "Witchcraft" with its subtly-projected sexuality, or the equally compelling, finger-snapping "Nice 'N' Easy".

Sinatra connoisseurs had a point when they protested at the recording of novelty songs such as "French Foreign Legion" and a hip updating of "Ol' Macdonald". Despite the complaints, though, he sung (and swung) them both in joyous fashion ... and they were both hits.

There was also a run of so-so movies – *Some Came Running* (1958), *Never So Few* (1959) and *Ocean's Eleven* (1960) – involving members of the so-called Clan (Dean Martin, Peter Lawford, Shirley MacLaine, Joey Bishop and Sammy Davis Jr), a group of self-indulgent friends, whose outrageous social life had begun to take up reams of space in newspapers and magazines. The antics of the Clan all too often bordered on the infantile and included, for example, barging-in on a legit live performance by Eddie Fisher, and a virtual take-over of the show.

At first, the media were amused. Then, faint amusement turned into a gathering tirade against Sinatra & Co. One columnist, in comparing the group to Humphrey Bogart's near-legendary Holmby Hills Rat Pack – of which Sinatra was actually a member – declared that at least its predecessor kept its collective doings reasonably private: the Clan preferred to go public with its flamboyant antics. Sinatra's riposte was, simply, that the Clan was "a figment of someone's imagination". In fact, he added, they were merely a group of friends who met to enjoy each other's company.

On a more personal note, and in a twelve-part series on Sinatra, columnist Al Aronowitz of the *New York Post* described the singer as "the new King and Dictator of Hollywood" – an indication of the kind of power the once-rejected superstar now commanded in movie land. Aronowitz did not neglect to take the opportunity to comment on the activities of the Clan. And Richard Gehman in *Good Housekeeping* called Sinatra "the most feared man in Hollywood".

Frank Sinatra again made headlines during 1960 over his hiring of Albert Maltz to write the screenplay for a proposed production of *The Execution Of Private Slovik*, based on William Bradford Huie's study of the only soldier to be executed by the US Army since the Civil War. Controversy arose because Maltz was one of the so-called Hollywood Ten, who had been convicted of contempt of Congress in 1950, during the appalling days of McCarthyism. *Slovik* would have been the first movie project, under his own name, since his release from prison in April 1951. At first, Sinatra stood his ground in the face of increasing hostility from both the Hearst press and a strong Right-wing element in Hollywood itself headed by John Wayne. He insisted he would stand by his principles, and that "… in my role as a picture-maker, I have – in my opinion – hired the best man to do the job".

Sadly, it was not to be. Less than three weeks later, a statement was issued from Sinatra's home in Palm Springs stating that Maltz had been relieved of the post and a settlement had been made, and ending, "I will accept the majority opinion."

To this day, Hollywood has not made up its collective mind about the rights or wrongs of Sinatra's final decision. For many, opposed to the feelings of Wayne & Co, the situation was summarised perfectly by a contributor to *Publishers' Weekly*, "Chalk up another victory for the lynch-law mentality."

In September 1960, Nancy Jr wed rock'n'rolling Tommy Sands in Vegas. She was given away by her father. The year ended with Sinatra and Lawford still working out final details for the Inaugural Gala, the following month. The Film Exhibitors of America selected Sinatra and Elizabeth Taylor as the year's top box office stars. And *McCall's* included him. among their 24 top personalities as one of the Most Attractive Men in the World.

Playback time: with Juliet Prowse, FS, Sammy Cahn and Felix Slatkin.

At this time, however, there was one particular event above all other items in a non-stop schedule which Sinatra was looking forward to with typical determination.

Not only was he on the point of severing his association with Capitol Records in the New Year, but the idea was he would soon be presiding over his own brand-new record company. Having already completed no less than three of his own albums, plus sundry singles, he was thus well prepared for this new venture.

Poignantly, his last Capitol album – titled appropriately, *Point Of No Return* – was made with arranger/conductor Axel Stordahl, who showed that he had lost none of his creative genius. It was a timely recall, too, for this warm, friendly and eminently talented man died, at his home in Encino, California, after a long illness, at the dreadfully young age of 50 in August 1963.

Sinatra's very last Capitol session took place on March 6, 1962, by which time his own record company, Reprise, was well and truly in business. The session was a strictly one-number affair, with Bill Miller producing and Swing Era veteran Skip Martin providing the arrangement.

It has never been revealed since why Sinatra bowed out with an old Harold Arlen standard he'd never recorded before. Maybe there was a message in its title, taped especially for his former employers. The song was "I Gotta Right To Sing The Blues" …

Cahn, Van Heusen, Lawford, Sinatra, listen to "High Hopes" (re-written à la JFK).

1953-1960

RECORDS

APART FROM THE occasional slip-up, it can justifiably be said that the Fifties

resulted in Sinatra's greatest body of recorded work. It wasn't as if the Capitol

albums and singles obliterated everything that had gone before (on Columbia), or

denied much of what was to come later (on Reprise), but, in terms of quantity and

quality, the Capitol years were Sinatra's Golden Years.

Even in the Nineties, it's hard to deny that most of Sinatra's Capitol material

still cuts the mustard. While many of his contemporaries sound dated, **_Swingin' Session!_**
A rare Sinatra
Sinatra's recordings have stood up well to the passage of time. **_failure on_**
Capitol.

Naturally, staying power was what Capitol were hoping for when they put their faith in a singer, whose career seemed to be over – and Sinatra's solid commercial success has repaid the company many times over.

From the start, Sinatra provided Capitol with a regular stream of major single hits, like "Three Coins In The Fountain", "Young At Heart", "The Tender Trap" and "Love And Marriage" [all on _This Is Frank Sinatra 1953-57_].

And even when some single releases didn't quite click with the record-buyers, their quality was more often than not outstanding. One immediately thinks of such eloquent titles as "Rain (Falling From The Sky)", "My One And Only Love", "The Gal That Got Away" and "Something Wonderful Happens In Summer" [all on _This Is Frank Sinatra 1953-57_].

In the early days of the long-playing record, Sinatra became the standard-setter with _Songs For Young Lovers_, his first Capitol

album and the public's first in-depth taste of the "new" Frank Sinatra. There may have been superior versions of songs such as "Like Someone In Love", "A Foggy Day" or "My Funny Valentine", but it's hard to think of any.

The same can be said for so many of the subsequent Capitol sets. *Close To You* and *Songs For Swingin' Lovers*, in their different moods, offer the same track-by-track quality. All the prime assets in Sinatra's legendary vocal equipment were brought to bear on *Close To You*: the diction, phrasing, breath-control, the pauses, and a marvellously-controlled yet heartfelt emotion. "PS I Love You",

a charming Mercer-Jenkins collaboration, takes pride-of-place. This is the art of vocal conversation at its peak.

Songs For Swingin' Lovers contains not one repeat. There is such an exhilarating, uplifting mood about the whole album that track-by-track inspection might lead the listener to believe that no better versions of the 15 (or, with the addition later of "Memories Of You", 16) numbers could exist anywhere. In Sinatra's hands, every song took on a whole new meaning. "I've Got You Under My Skin" had never really been a significant opus in Cole Porter's catalogue: *Swingin' Lovers* (and Sinatra) put it on the map, for all time ...

Swingin' Lovers remains many peoples' Number 1 all-time favourite album – since its first release in the UK in 1956, it has in all probability never been absent from the Capitol catalogue. There are those, however, who believe that it is possibly inferior to its "swingin'" successor, *A Swingin' Affair*. The 15 rhythmic tracks here comprise an interesting repertoire, including Ellington's "I Got It Bad", and "From This Moment On", "Night And Day" (Sinatra's third recording) and the often underrated "At Long Last Love", all from the pen of Cole Porter. As appealing as are the majority of the "swingin'" albums, one has to search through the ballad collections for the definitive Frank Sinatra, such as *Close To You*, or *In The Wee Small Hours*, or *Only The Lonely* – each masterminded with keen attention to detail by Nelson Riddle.

But the two Jenkins sets also touched the heights. *Where Are You?* makes for absorbing listening, at anytime; year by year, it seems to become more meaningful, more vital. Once again, there is not a weak link in this skilful chain of emotional singing-arranging-playing Perhaps the recapitulation of "I'm A Fool To Want You" lacks the rawness of the Columbia version, but it is a masterpiece nevertheless. The most memorable track of all is a reading of "Autumn Leaves", which is like no other. Haunting, yes; emotive, certainly. But even more than these qualities, Sinatra's unfolding of Johnny Mercer's English lyric produces an aura of mystery that at times borders on the surrealistic.

Not only does this moving version of "Autumn Leaves" rank with the singer's most compelling performances on record. It is so extraordinary, there is absolutely no chance of anyone else equalling, let alone surpassing, it.

In The Wee Small Hours has been the musicians' choice since it first appeared in 1955. Each of the songs seems to have been hand-picked. Some, like the exquisitely-phrased "Dancing On The Ceiling", "I'll Be Around" (with its supreme control) and "Glad To Be Unhappy" (Sinatra here matching cynicism with his own brand of home-spun philosophy) have accompaniments provided by a simple four- or five-piece rhythm section. Elsewhere, Riddle has furnished inspiring but never intrusive "symphonic" scores. It seems almost churlish to select further highlights from the rest, but Sinatra's interpretations of "Deep

A stylish, relaxed Sinatra, characteristics of his output during the Captiol years.

In A Dream", "In The Wee Small Hours Of The Morning", "I Get Along Without You Very Well" and, finest of all the 15 cuts, a magisterial "Last Night When We Were Young" – the final word, surely, on Harold Arlen's magnum opus – are matchless.

Three years on, *Only The Lonely* (1958) was if anything, more emotional than *In The Wee Small Hours*. The voice is coarser, certainly; but this adds even more depth to the interpretation. And Nelson Riddle never wrote more feelingly. "Spring Is Here", "Willow, Weep For Me", "Blues In The Night", "What's New?" and "Gone With The Wind" – thanks to the combined efforts of Sinatra and Riddle, each one sounded like a brand-new number. The sadly-neglected "It's A Lonesome Old Town" simply defines loneliness, with no high-flown drama; both "Angel Eyes" and "One For My Baby" are the finest of Sinatra's favourite saloon-song performances.

Songs For Young Lovers and *Come Fly With Me* represent the finest of the eclectic albums. The latter benefits from Billy May's first charts for Sinatra. Their coming-together produces a series of flamboyant performances, epitomized by the Cahn-Van Heusen title tune, plus an hilarious re-creation of Kipling's "(On The) Road To Mandalay", as well as uplifting collaborations on "Let's Get Away From It All" and "It's Nice To Go Trav'ling" (more new Cahn-Van Heusen). The irresistibility of the swingers is complemented by a series of superior ballad selections. "London By Night" and "Autumn In New York" are merely excellent; "April In Paris" and "Moonlight In Vermont" are near-flawless ... even by Sinatra's greatest balladeering standards.

Young Lovers is even more of an all-round masterpiece than *Come Fly With Me*. Each of its eight titles sees Sinatra at his peak. The swingers – scored expertly by George Siravo – find the singer as close to jazz as anywhere on record, with "A Foggy Day" and "I Get A Kick Out Of You" at the top of the pile; the same goes for the ballads, "My Funny Valentine" and "Like Someone In Love". Such was Sinatra's omnipotence during the Fifties, that even collections comprising single releases or out-cuts, such as *This Is Sinatra*, *This Is Sinatra, Volume Two* and *Look To Your Heart* – [All on *This Is Frank Sinatra 1953-1957*] – tend to sound like single-album productions in their own right.

Ultimately, though, it was to be Sinatra's thematic albums which were to pass into pop-music lore.

MOVIES

EVEN NOW, it's hard to say whether it was movies or recordings which played the bigger part in reviving Frank Sinatra's career in the period following *From Here To Eternity*.

Certainly, there's no doubt that Sinatra's re-emergence as a movie star helped him immeasurably in becoming the biggest name in show business, especially since he was now considered a "serious" actor of real stature. Indeed, many of the fans who materialized during the Fifties – the most significant decade of Sinatra's career – were first drawn by his appearances on the silver screen and only later became interested in the man's music.

Sinatra's Maggio in *From Here To Eternity* captured the imaginations of committed cinema-goers as well as casual film fans and the impact of the Academy Award, which followed, reverberated throughout Hollywood and the entertainment industry. Sinatra's period in the doldrums was over – suddenly he was able to pick and choose what work he wanted ... even though Maggio would remain, forever, his movie milestone.

Even before the applause had died away, Sinatra had taken on a leading role in *Suddenly* (1954), portraying a sadistic, would-be Presidential assassin with a conviction that riveted the attention ... he'd learnt a lot from Montgomery Clift. Critical acclaim for this role proved that Sinatra's acting in *Eternity* had been no fluke.

Left: As Frankie Machine in *The Man With The Golden Arm*. Background: With Edward G. Robinson in *A Hole in The Head*.

From this point on, Sinatra's career in motion pictures was on the up. True there was at least one real disaster – *Johnny Concho* (1956), a brave attempt to make the main character in a Western (played by first-time producer Sinatra) an out-and-out coward – but, for the most part, Sinatra's films continued to triumph.

The heady mixture of nine major movies that followed *Eternity* included dramatic parts for Sinatra in all manner of non-singing productions, out-and-out musicals, films which called for both acting and singing, plus comedy "within a musical context".

Throughout, Sinatra continued to demonstrate top-grade acting, most notably as a heroin-addicted card dealer in *The Man With The Golden Arm* (1955) and, two years later, with his portrayal of alcoholic night-club comedian, Joe E Lewis, in *The Joker Is Wild*.

Sinatra's stand-out performance as Frankie Machine in an otherwise disappointing *Golden Arm* hit the mark perfectly. The high spot was a lengthy scene with Machine alone in a locked bedroom, trying to kick his long-time drug habit. Apparently, its realistic quality stemmed from a period the actor spent closely observing junkies' withdrawal symptoms in a controlled hospital situation. A second Oscar nomination came as no surprise but ultimately the award for Best Actor went to Ernest Borgnine.

1957 was the year in which Sinatra completed three full-length movies, so it came as a shock when he failed to receive a single nomination at the relevant Academy Awards, especially for his acting-singing contributions to *The Joker Is Wild*. Still Sinatra must have been pleased that his song writing buddies, Sammy Cahn and Jimmy Van Heusen, copped Best Song honours for "All The Way", the picture's "big" number.

Pal Frankie – Book-ended, but not bewitched, by Hayworth and Novak.

The star could also console himself with the fact that it was his acting which dominated a fine, atmospheric production. As for the soundtrack, apart from a first-time version of "All The Way", Sinatra's performances of standards such as "I Cried For You" and "If I Could Be With You One Hour Tonight" are less than totally successful. [*The Soundtrack Sessions*] Although jazz-based vocals provided an appropriate "period" feel and style, his attempts at swinging in 2/4 simply weren't convincing – with the exception of

"Chicago". The truth is Sinatra has always been a 4/4 performer ...

Pal Joey (1957), predictably, presented no such problems for Sinatra. Showing a fine comedic talent witnessed previously in *The Tender Trap* (also 1957), he was in peak vocal form taking on an all-Rodgers/Hart score.

No one cares in *The Joker Is Wild*. Singer Joe E. Lewis, his vocal cords cut by the Mob, is in despair.

Sadly, apart from songs such as "Bewitched" and "I Could Write A Book", this wasn't the score from the original Broadway smash-hit production. Gone were several delightful numbers, including some of Hart's most witty and inventive lyrics (e.g. "Take Him"; "Happy Hunting Horn"; "In Our Little Den Of Iniquity"), while other gems ("You Mustn't Kick It Around"; "Plant You Now, Dig You Later"; "Do It The Hard Way") were relegated to mere background music for on-screen club sequences.

For the dedicated Sinatra fan, however, there is much to savour. His elegant readings of "Bewitched" and "I Could Write A Book", from the stage version, and "I Didn't Know What Time It Was", as well as "There's A Small Hotel" (from two other R&H Broadway musicals) were well up to par, and this screen version of "The Lady Is A Tramp", yet another import, produced a truly electrifying performance.

The scene where Sinatra "serenades" Rita Hayworth in an after-hours performance at a night-club remains, forever, his single most exhilarating musical performance of all his 25 motion-picture appearances containing any kind of musical content.

The remainder of Sinatra's film work in the Fifties was an interesting mixture to say the least. There were a couple of other strong non-musical productions – *Not As A Stranger* (1955), with Sinatra shaping up to strong acting competition from Robert Mitchum, Broderick Crawford and Charles Bickford, and *A Hole In The Head* (1959), with Edward G Robinson heading an even more impressive cast that included the likes of Thelma Ritter, Eleanor Parker, Keenan Wynn and Carolyn Jones. This production also featured the Oscar-winning "High Hopes" as well as the dreadfully underrated "All My Tomorrows", sung beautifully off-screen, over the credits, by Sinatra.

Both *High Society* (1956) and *Young At Heart* (1955) contained more fine vocals. The former featured Sinatra's debut

Hand in hand with Debbie Reynolds (far left) in *The Tender Trap*, and being taken for a ride by a future Princess of Monaco Grace Kelly, in the all-time classic *High Society*.

alongside his mentor, Bing Crosby – their marvellous duet on "Well, Did You Evah?" was the musical highlight and the Cole Porter score presented Sinatra with the finest solo item, "You're Sensational", sung to an inebriated Grace Kelly.

High Society was a remake-with-music of *The Philadelphia Story*, a justly-celebrated comedy from 1940. *Young At Heart*, likewise, was a remake with musical interpolations of *Four Daughters* (1938). Sinatra's embittered-and-cynical songwriter, and sometime singer-pianist, dominates *Young At Heart*. Apart from the charming title tune, Sinatra's versions of a trio of top standards ("Someone To Watch Over Me"; "Just One Of Those Things"; "One For My Baby") are peerless.

***Guys And Dolls*:**

Marlon Brando –
"Betcha don't know
what color tie you're
wearin'."
Francis A – "Now you
come to mention it. I
ain't sure either."

Sinatra desperately wanted the role of Sky Masterson in Frank Loesser's marvellously inventive, well-nigh perfect musical, *Guys And Dolls* (1955). Unfortunately, Marlon Brando got the part and Sinatra had to make do with Nathan Detroit. Much like

Pal Joey, Hollywood (in the shape of the redoubtable Samuel Goldwyn, one imagines) decreed that the score for the screen-recreation of this Broadway masterpiece had to lose some songs. That didn't prevent Sinatra from doing full justice to "Sue Me" (in tandem with Vivian Blaine) and "Adelaide", then sharing an equally joyous "Guys And Dolls" and "The Oldest Established (Permanent Floating Crap Game In New York)" with Stubby Kaye and Johnny Silver, in buoyant fashion.

The tail-end of the Fifties saw a succession of mainly non-singing roles. Results were variable – *Kings Go Forth* (1958) was average World War II fare; *Some Came Running* (1958), with Sinatra cast as a would-be author, was marginally better and the first of the Rat Pack movies; meanwhile *Never So Few* (1959) was a bore with Sinatra unconvincing as a US Army officer in Burma…

The year 1960 heralded a whole new decade of Sinatra-at-the-movies. It started modestly enough. Cole Porter's *Can-Can* (1960) found him slightly uneasy as a French lawyer, François Durnais, co-starring with Shirley MacLaine (with whom he duetted earnestly on "Let's Do It"), Maurice Chevalier (another duet – "Montmart'") and Louis Jourdan. The highlight of a rather disappointing production was Sinatra's flawless interpretation of "It's All Right With Me", which the singer wisely opted to perform as a straight ballad – strictly out-of-tempo – extracting every ounce of meaning from a superior lyric and producing what is probably the finest version ever of the song.

Ocean's Eleven (1960), featuring a squad of Rat Pack regulars in a plot about former wartime colleagues robbing five gambling casinos in Las Vegas simultaneously on New Year's Eve, was an entertaining, if unimportant, picture that did well at the box office.

These films were a reasonable start to the Sixties for a major movie star of Sinatra's status and prefaced Sinatra's continued strong involvement in this, the biggest money-making area of all his professional activities.

TELEVISION

IT TOOK Frank Sinatra much longer than most of his contemporaries to establish himself as a contributor to the medium of television.

Other than the odd guest-spot, his initial involvement came during the "dark days" between 1950 and 1951 with the first-ever *Frank Sinatra Show*. The series was less than an overwhelming success and somehow its host never really looked the part on the small screen – the beginning of the Fifties wasn't exactly peak Sinatra in terms of vocal projection.

After *From Here To Eternity*, Sinatra plunged into hectic movie-making and record-making; any spare time he had was set aside for gigs. Of course, there were rare appearances on TV but, by the mid-Fifties, Sinatra had become unenthusiastic about this fastest-growing section of the media. Indeed, he was known to sound off against it in no uncertain terms.

In 1955, Sinatra told A E Hotchner, of the Canadian *Redbook* magazine, "Man, I've seen (TV) chew up a lot of talent from a lot of great people. Let's face it, I'm not fond of TV. It takes too much energy, too much tension, havoc and rehearsals for the results you get. I know what it can do to your inside. I had a one-hour weekly show for CBS for a whole year. The only guy I know who has survived and made it pay is Ed Sullivan – the modern Rudy Vallee. Ed is making profit out of 1905 vaudeville! Show him Fink's mules and he'll grab 'em and put 'em out there ..."

But Sinatra reserved his most caustic comments for the people who ran US television, "My blood boils when I see the mediocrities who are sitting at the top of the TV networks; refugees from ad agencies who think that show business is stuck together with spit and gimmicks ... In TV, mediocrities have inherited the earth."

It took until 1957 before a brand new *Frank Sinatra Show* was unveiled again. Indeed, the show business world pricked up its ears when the ABC network announced that Frank Sinatra had signed a three-year contract to star in his own TV specials – the original plan was for 13 half-hour musical and 13 half-hour drama productions. The series began on October 18 and included two live hour-long specials with Chesterfield Cigarettes as sponsors. For his not inconsiderable services, the star performer received a cheque for a cool $3 million.

However, the critics didn't exactly rave about the opening show, which had guest spots for Bob Hope, Peggy Lee and Kim Novak. There were no complaints about the host's singing – hard-swinging performances of "The Lonesome Road", "I Get A Kick Out Of You" and 'The Lady Is A Tramp"; superior ballad-singing on "I Could Write A Book", 'All The Way", "Bewitched" and a touching "Autumn Leaves". The criticisms were about the show itself and its general concept. "Banal", shouted one reviewer, while another felt the attempts at humour were less than successful.

It wasn't a happy augury for the future. By November, ratings had dipped. But the show survived until the following May. By this time, Chesterfield had withdrawn sponsorship and the final three transmissions came courtesy of Bulova. Watched years later, the dialogue sounds contrived, the humour forced; the non-musical sections were at best throwaway additions. On the positive side, the guest roster was usually up to the mark. Visiting vocalists included Dinah Shore, Keely Smith, Ethel Merman, Ella Fitzgerald, Jo Stafford, Bing Crosby and Rat Pack buddies, Dean Martin and Sammy Davis Jr.

Rehearsin's so cool. While Frank takes his ease, Dino goes for a shoe-shine.

Musically, Sinatra's contributions were near-flawless. Picking performances at random, there were impeccable versions of "Taking A Chance On Love", "PS I Love You", "Witchcraft", "There's No You" and "I'm Gonna Live Till I Die" - each from different transmissions in 1958. But somehow his attempts at making the show acutely hip (Sinatra style) struck the wrong note for a TV audience.

But the demise of the show didn't mark the end of Sinatra-on-TV. In mid-1959, he was contracted to complete a quartet of one-hour specials, once more to be networked by ABC. On these, Sinatra was more relaxed and at ease. His singing was impressive too, including a pulsating "Too Marvellous For Words" taken at near-jet tempo (from the second of the shows) and a truly forlorn "Lonely Town" (from the third). Yet, sadly, it was only the fourth, and last, special which really picked up top ratings. *Welcome Home, Elvis* was the title. Demobbed from the army, the high-profile,

Left: Sinatra with Louis Armstrong.

The Voice greets the Pelvis, 1966. Elvis invested "Witchcraft" with one of his classic pelvic rotations.

once again plain Mr Presley was the centre of attraction – even though, Sinatra, Sammy Davis Jr, Peter Lawford, Joey Bishop and daughter Nancy all turned up at the Fontainebleau, Miami, to celebrate. Presley got the chance to do "Stuck On You" and "Fame And Fortune". And he joined the show's host for a duet which found the latter projecting "Love Me Tender" as a mid-tempo swinger, with Presley attempting a rock-tinged "Witchcraft".

Sinatra's appearance on the expensive *Edsel* show (presented by the Ford Motor Company and transmitted in mid-October, 1957) found him in easy-going, wisecracking form, in the congenial company of Bing Crosby, Rosemary Clooney and Louis Armstrong (with Bob Hope making a brief cameo). The highlight was "The Birth Of The Blues", a rousing, warm duet between Sinatra and Armstrong.

Perhaps the most interesting of Sinatra's TV appearances in the late Fifties/early Sixties came in September 1955. A 90-minute production of Thornton Wilder's play *Our Town*, also starring Paul Newman and Eva Marie Saint, it was one Sinatra appearance that was greeted with unanimous critical praise. The songs were in the capable hands of Cahn and Van Heusen and all the leads got the chance to sing. Sinatra himself sang the introductory "Our Town", then "The Impatient Years', "Love And Marriage" and, finally, "Look To Your Heart". He recorded all four titles for Capitol and, of course, the third-named became a major hit.

Made as part of a *Producer's Showcase* series, *Our Town* was a one-off production, never to be repeated. Sinatra later expressed the opinion that the play "had a lot of merit" – although he didn't feel four weeks of solid rehearsals justified the end result. "I could make a good movie in that time," he told A E Hotchner.

Songwriter Sammy Cahn was proud to be associated with *Our Town*. As he told this writer 20 years later, "It was an incredible adventure, because it's testimony to the man's audacity ... It went on air at six o'clock in California – nine o'clock, New York time... Director Delbert Mann, in the control booth, pointed a finger – and the show went out. Live. No taping... Nelson Riddle was in a studio across the street. Frank was singing 'Look To Your Heart' to Nelson through loudspeakers ... it was a real breakthrough ... "

RADIO

BY THE MID-FIFTIES, Sinatra's involvement with live radio was over. His other commitments, together with the fact that TV was gradually overwhelming its nearest rival, meant that the halcyon days of *Your Hit Parade*, *Songs By Sinatra* and *Light-Up Time* were becoming memories of the past. His last important series was *To Be Perfectly Frank*, which lasted from November 1953 until April 1955, by which time it was being aired only sporadically.

Broadcast, for the first year at least, twice-weekly, this 15-minutes slot showcased Sinatra, accompanied by a five-piece combo, singing a wide range of material. Bearing in mind the dates of recording and transmission, this was Sinatra at his veritable peak. He sang ballads with great control and depth, then swung the rhythmic numbers with a poise and assurance rarely repeated in later years. As well as the "new" songs, the programmes often included commercial recordings – by Sinatra himself, including both current and pre-Capitol discs, plus offerings by Pearl Bailey, Lena Horne, Louis Armstrong, Frankie Laine, Jimmie Lanceford and Les Brown, among others.

Apart from the impressive consistency of his live singing throughout the series, a notable point of interest was hearing Sinatra re-work old favourites, giving completely fresh dimensions to his interpretations.

Even more intriguing was the inclusion of standards he would never, at any time during his career, record for any label. Among the swingers were "What Can I Say After I Say I'm Sorry?", "If I Could Be With You One Hour Tonight", "'S'Wonderful", "Between The Devil And The Deep Blue Sea" and "Love Me Or Leave Me". And he often included the choicest of ballads –

"Tenderly", "Out Of Nowhere", "Don't Blame Me", "One Hundred Years From Today" and "I'm In The Mood For Love".

The *To Be Perfectly Frank* series, which was re-broadcast by the United States Armed Forces Radio And Television Service, was not only Sinatra's last series, but his most important. Thankfully, numerous individual performances have been made available through the years, including *Perfectly Frank* and as part of *Sinatra: The Radio Years 1939-1955*.

Sinatra's other radio series of the Fifties was *Rocky Fortune*. Twenty-five minutes in length, and with Sinatra in the title role, this was a weekly drama series networked by NBC and re-broadcast by AFRTS. It started in the fall of 1953 and ran for just over six months.

For British audiences, the pop highlight of 1953 must surely have been Sinatra's totally unexpected appearance – twice – on BBC radio, as special guest of *The Show Band Show*. Thanks to the combined efforts of Show Band-leader Cyril Stapleton and producer Johnnie Stewart, Sinatra appeared, first, on June 11. His singing must have astounded both studio audience and the general listening public, who had been led to believe for some time that, as a singer, he was completely over the hill.

Instead, his three-number programme – "Birth Of The Blues", "Ol' Man River" and "I'm Walking Behind You" – revealed a vocalist, who, far from being finished, was on the brink of even greater achievements. Something which his second appearance, a month later, comprehensively confirmed. On this occasion, he presented electrifying versions of "I've Got The World On A String", "Day In-Day Out" and 'London By Night", the memory of which lives forever in the minds of those fortunate enough to have heard the programme.

For the remainder of the decade, there was to be the odd appearance on radio by Frank Sinatra, mostly associated with short charity programmes. But British audiences did get an opportunity, late in 1958, to hear an edited version of the Monaco Gala Concert of June 14.

Forties radio fun: Frank and Bing go for laughs, while Hedy Lamarr and Hope remain unaware.

GIGS

If any doubt existed about Sinatra's ability as a supreme live performer, it was expunged forever during the Fifties. Sinatra had became the Complete Vocalist. His on-stage deportment, his matchless use of the hand-microphone (replacing the ugly, clumsy stand-up variety of earlier times), the force of his personality and the sheer conviction of his delivery, all combined to elevate his talent to a level of excellence that few could match.

Even though his constant movie-making and frequent visits to the recording studio kept down the number of live gigs, there are many who still recall the spellbinding performances he gave at this time.

Former Dorsey trombonist, Billy VerPlanck, is one. Husband of singer Marlene VerPlanck and a fine arranger in his own right, VerPlanck was a member of the orchestra led by brothers Jimmy and Tommy Dorsey, which accompanied Sinatra on-stage at the Paramount Theatre in August 1956. They were there for the premiere of the ill-fated movie, *Johnny Concho*. Sinatra played to capacity audiences, for a week, before the film was shown each night. Well, almost one week, as far as Sinatra was concerned – laryngitis took him out of three of the shows.

Sinatra was in sensational form, recalls VerPlanck. "He did a 26-number programme opening night, and it was one of the great moments of my career in music. Couldn't be better."

Like so many musicians who have worked with Sinatra, VerPlanck remembers too that rehearsals could be as memorable as the concerts themselves. "I mean, Nelson (Riddle) was on hand, to help. But it was Frank who really rehearsed the thing. It was absolutely wonderful. So musical ... and so absolutely right."
The following year found Sinatra with Riddle, playing a concert at the Civic Auditorium, in Seattle, Washington. Again, Sinatra was in superlative form throughout an hour-long programme comprising 18 numbers. The repertoire concentrated in the main on loosely-swinging readings of excerpts from the rhythmic Capitol albums - *Swingin' Lovers*, *Young Lovers* and the recently-completed *A Swingin' Affair*.

"Just One Of Those Things" (from *Swing Easy!*) benefited from being performed live; and both "You Make Me Feel So Young" and "I've Got You Under My Skin" were as rhythmically sound as any other concert versions. And, in Seattle, Sinatra presented probably his finest on-stage "Oh, Look At Me Now". The ballads were compressed into a five-number selection near the end. Best of these were "Glad To Be Unhappy" and "My Funny Valentine": in both cases, Sinatra managed to achieve an intimacy within the confines of a large concert hall that most other vocalists could only dream about.

The Sporting Club, in Monte Carlo, was the setting for yet another notable performance. Held in June 1958 in aid of the United Nations Refugee Fund, the event took place in front of a very upmarket audience, headed by their Serene Highnesses, Prince Rainier and the late Princess Grace of Monaco.

Noel Coward introduced the special guest in glowing terms – both in French and English, "Never once a breach of taste, never once a wrong note". And an obviously buoyant Sinatra treated the glitter-and-gold audience to 40 minutes of superb singing, plus some typical "rest-period" chat. "I've Got You Under My Skin" was projected in an even more overtly sexual way than usual ("We may all get arrested tonight!" he interpolated at one stage), and "Come Fly With Me" soared triumphantly. "Where Or When", sung mostly with just piano accompaniment, which he would record for Capitol in the same format, got a breathtaking treatment; and both "Moonlight In Vermont" and "April In Paris" went like a dream – the hangover phrases were carried through effortlessly.

But for many of the audience, Sinatra's idiosyncratic "(On The) Road To Mandalay" probably registered strongest. In terms of topicality, "Monique", a song inspired by *Kings Go Forth*, received its debut live performance – the Midnight Gala took place after the premiere of the movie [*Sinatra: Monte Carlo 14 June 1958*].

As exceptional as any of the concerts mentioned above was that which took place on April 1, 1959 at the West Melbourne Stadium in Australia – [*Vintage Sinatra, Vol. 2*]. The freewheeling Sinatra who thrilled the Aussies was accompanied by a five-man combo, fronted by vibist Red Norvo. From a spring-heeled opening "I Could Have Danced All Night", right through to as dynamic a "Night And Day" as he can ever have performed live, Sinatra was at his most electrifying. Altogether, 50 minutes of Sinatra magic ...

In terms of flawless singing, from start to finish, those fortunate enough to be present at a Sinatra appearance at the 500 Club, Atlantic City [*The Sinatra Saga*], still rave, some 35 years later. Opening with a whirlwind "Too Marvellous For Words", his performance, as one member of the audience remembers, "was like no other in-person appearance I can recall. There were times, I swear, when he seemed like a guy possessed. He did 'I Could Have Danced All Night' – we all were sure he could've sung all night!"

Jim Biddulph, a retired businessman from Philadelphia, is sure that "there were versions of several of the tunes – 'Too Marvellous' was one, 'Moonlight In Vermont' and 'All the Way' were others – that he just cannot have sung better. At anytime ..."

Doing it *his* way? Sinatra in charge at rehearsals, telling the guys what he needs at showtime.

The Reprise Years

"To play & play again"... but not forever?

LEGEND HAS IT that in December 1960 Frank Sinatra passed by the new and impressive Capitol Tower building in Hollywood with record company executive, Mo Ostin. He turned to Ostin and said,

"I helped to build that. Now, let's build one of my own."

The following year, the dream of running his own record label had become reality. And throughout the Sixties, though there was to be no let-up in Sinatra's movie-making and television activities, it was primarily Reprise Records which would continue to keep its founder and first boss in the spotlight.

From the outset, Sinatra was determined to build up a strong roster of talent. During 1962, Reprise's first year in business, Sammy Davis Jr, Dean Martin, Jimmy Witherspoon and Sinatra's eldest daughter, Nancy then aged 20, were among those who became affiliated to the new label. Soon Bing Crosby, Count Basie and Nelson Riddle were to sign up too.

Sinatra on Reprise – some disappointments maybe, but his recordings for the label did not lack variety.

Sinatra offered his artists the kind of arrangement he himself had sought from Capitol: each of them was to retain ownership of their recording masters; they would organize their own sessions; and there were no restrictions on their involvement with other record companies.

For Frank Sinatra and many of his contemporaries, the Sixties proved frustrating. Record companies, large and small, were concentrating their efforts on catering to the youth market, which was growing at an astounding rate. Non-rock artists came under pressure to conform.

However, apart from the single "Everybody's Twistin'", Sinatra maintained an unswerving indifference to changing styles. At first, the Reprise label had virtually no hits in the singles market, but something had to give.

Thanks to Sammy Davis, a breakthrough occurred in late 1962 with "What Kind Of Fool Am I?", which got into the Top 20. Then came a Top Five for Reprise, also in 1962, with comedian Lou Monte's less-than-scintillating "Pepino – The Italian Mouse". Exactly a year later, a young Texan, Trini Lopez, became the highest-placed Reprise artist so far, when "If I Had A Hammer" rocketed to No 3. It was Dean Martin, though, who really put Reprise on the map with "Everybody Loves Somebody" – an old Sinatra song! – which went to the top of the US Hit Parade.

Survival was ensured late in 1963, when Warner's chief, Jack L Warner, agreed to purchase two-thirds of Reprise Records. The deal brought Sinatra Enterprises under the Warner umbrella with one-third of Warner Bros Records falling into Sinatra's possession.

Four years later, Sinatra sold a further 13 percent of Reprise to Warner-Seven Arts for $4,200,000; the remaining 20 percent he sold to Kinney National Service, which itself would eventually take over Warner-Seven Arts (in March, 1969) for a further $22,500,000 in cash and convertible debentures. In total, it is estimated, Sinatra received around $80 million for his record company.

In order that the newly-created Reprise division of Warner Bros. Records should start making real money, its 1961-63 roster was drastically pruned. Former MGM, now Reprise, executive Mo Ostin initiated the signing of new artists, with the emphasis this time placed on an ever-broadening rock horizon.

Even more ambitious, perhaps, was Warners' view that Sinatra, Martin and other older-generation artists could make their mark in the rock and pop market - as part of a "soft-rock" division. With a view to bringing them back into the singles charts, newcomers, producer Jimmy Bowen and arranger Ernie Freeman, were assigned to work on both Martin and Sinatra.

By the Sixties, Sinatra live was second to none – *the* consummate vocal performer.

Freeman in particular took a lot of stick from critics for the kind of pop charts he produced for Sinatra. Nonetheless, the very first Sinatra-Freeman-Bowen collaboration produced a beautifully-felt version of "Softly, As I Leave You", with big-band brass-reeds, plus strings, with classic rock triplets in the chart and drummer Hal Blaine laying down a basic beat in prescribed soft-rock style.

Success in re-establishing Frank Sinatra as a major pop singer took rather longer than had been imagined. The song that wrought the change – and what a change! – in Sinatra's fortunes was a tune by German band leader Bert Kaempfert, with English lyrics by Charles Singleton and Eddie Snyder.

A good, if by no means outstanding, performance by Sinatra of an ordinary number, "Strangers In The Night" received massive airplay on all but the heaviest rock stations in the States. In practically no time, it was topping the charts in the US and the UK. It went on to make the Number 1 position in four other territories around the world. In fact, it was the biggest single hit Frank Sinatra would ever achieve – bigger than anything from the Columbia or Capitol eras.

For Sinatra, it was not just an important breakthrough. It opened the flood-gates. Back-catalogue album material took on a new life. And the new album – predictably entitled *Strangers In The Night* – sold prodigiously, even though it scarcely ranked as an artistic masterpiece. Still, not only was it the biggest-selling Sinatra LP on Reprise, it was his first chart-topper since *Nice'N'Easy* in 1960. And there was a further hit single during 1966, the gutsy, R&B-based "That's Life". As if that wasn't enough, during this halcyon period, Frank, duetting with daughter Nancy, saw "Somethin' Stupid" become a mega-hit of 1967.

A couple of years on, the song destined to become the Sinatra anthem was released. Of French origin and titled "Comme d'Habitude", it was written by Jacques Revaux, Claude François and Gilles Thibout. In 1967, former teenage pop idol, Paul Anka,

penned English lyrics and "My Way", retitled and published by Anka, rapidly became a modern standard (covered by, among others, Elvis Presley, Dorothy Squires and even Sid Vicious, plus Anka himself).

Curiously, "My Way" was never a massive hit for Sinatra in the US, but it achieved extraordinary popularity among British record-buyers. Whereas it just squeezed into the Top 30 in Sinatra's own country, its chart longevity in the UK was astounding. Following its initial entry on 2 April 1969, it remained in the charts, on and off, for nearly three years. *Nine* chart entries in all. No other record – by any other artist, at any time – has ever made such an impact on a singles chart.

On the personal front, there were several events during the Sixties which caused Sinatra genuine grief and deep-down pain. The assassinations of the Kennedy brothers and Martin Luther King hit him badly. In particular, he rated Jack Kennedy as a personal friend – even though his aspirations to become a regular White House visitor never materialized.

Sinatra was also shaken to the core by the death of his father, at the age of 74 from a combination of a major heart condition and emphysema. Those close to Sinatra insisted they'd never seen him as emotionally distraught. Other deaths that caused him distress during the decade were those of Marilyn Monroe, Spencer Tracy and his former press agent, Mark Millar.

The omens for 1963 were good, but pride and delight would soon be followed by shock and near-despair.

Frank Sinatra Jr made an unbilled debut appearance with the resident orchestra at Disneyland in 1962 and gigs which followed included a season at the plush Royal Box of Manhattan's Americana Hotel in September 1963. To Sinatra's delight, Junior's reviews were mostly favourable. Three months later came the event which caused such distress to his father, family and friends.

Junior was appearing in Vegas, again, this time at the Harrah's Lake Tahoe Casino. On Sunday, 8 December, he and a colleague were dining in Sinatra's motel room, prior to the first show of the evening. Pretending to be room service, two men gained entry to the premises. One threatened the pair with a revolver. His accomplice bound and gagged Sinatra's colleague, while the young singer was blindfolded, then forced into a waiting car. Frank Jr had been kidnapped.

Almost a day after the abduction, Sinatra Sr received a phone call to say that Junior was alive. On instruction, Sinatra drove to Carson City and a ransom sum was mentioned. Eventually, he was told to wait at Nancy's residence, in Bel-Air.

Next, Sinatra was ordered to leave $240,000, in cash inside a telephone booth at Los Angeles Airport. From there, he was redirected to a service station outside LA, then, to a Texaco station, in a completely different direction. Finally, he was told to leave the case full of dough in between two parked school buses. Sinatra didn't deposit the cash – this task was performed by an FBI agent. By this time, it was Wednesday ...

A call to Nancy stated that Junior would be released at an overpass at the Mulholland and San Diego Freeway. Dad left, in great haste, by car, accompanied by Federal agents. They returned, just over 30 minutes later ... alone.

The kidnap of Frank Jr brought his father close to despair. Shortly afterwards, a private policeman, driving in Bel-Air, was hailed by a young man, with a blindfold hanging limply around his neck. He recognized Frank Sinatra Jr. The young man and his family were reunited at three the following morning. Father's 48th birthday, the next day, turned out to be rather more of a celebration than had been planned.

(By Saturday, the FBI had arrested three men. Each was bailed at $50,000. After trial at the US District Court of Los Angeles, the following March, two of the kidnappers received life imprisonment, plus 75 years; the third received a lesser sentence – he'd been kind to Junior – of 16 years, eight months.)

Sinatra Sr found himself in real danger the following February. During the shooting of *None But The Brave*, a World War II pic, on Kauai, one of a small group of Hawaiian islands, he narrowly escaped drowning. While bathing offshore, he was engulfed by a huge wave at Wailua Bay and was soon in serious trouble.

Brad Dexter, an experienced film actor – and member of the cast – dived into the surf after Sinatra. A strong swimmer, Dexter just got to the fast-fading star, who by this time was suffering from hypoxia.

Sinatra's gratitude to Dexter was shown by the latter's immediate acceptance into the exclusive small-knit community of Frank's friends. He also gave Dexter a substantial part in his next movie, *Von Ryan's Express*. And Dexter's debut as screen producer came under Sinatra's auspices, two years later (1967), with *The Naked Runner*. It was the last occasion the pair would work together. Friendship between them ended when Dexter, it has been reported, said he could no longer take Sinatra's temperamental outbursts.

Frank Sinatra's marriage to the *gamine* Mia Farrow provided one of the gossip-columnists' favourite leads - even months before the actual event, which took place on 19 July 1966. Once again, as romance developed, the cynics sharpened their knives. After all, wasn't she a slim-line 19 when the couple first met (on the set of *Von Ryan's Express*) and wasn't he almost 50? Despite the general thumbs-down from those in the know, the pair grew fonder of each other as the months passed by.

The wedding ceremony took place at the Sands Hotel. The hotel's boss, Jack Entratter, acted as one of the witnesses before the couple left for their honeymoon in New York, London and Cap d'Antibes. Despite continued pessimism in some quarters, the marriage began to take shape. But the liaison lasted only 16 months.

It was Sinatra who started divorce proceedings. His wife was heartbroken. Ultimately, though, he persuaded Mia to seek a quick divorce. **A tense moment for Sinatra in *The Naked Runner*.**

This, she did – with great reluctance – in Juarez, Mexico. The date: 16 August 1968.

Throughout the Sixties, Sinatra kept falling out with people. Another break-up of a personal (and business) relationship had occurred in 1963. This was the split between Frank and his long-time buddy and business associate Hank Sanicola, just after the former had had his gaming licence revoked by the Nevada Gaming Board. The pair rowed and Sinatra rarely spoke to Sanicola again.

Charisma,
communication, class:
Sinatra displayed all
these characteristics in
the Sixties, in concert,
on disc and on
television.

■ 1 2 8

There was also a fall-out between Sinatra and Lena Horne. Their joint appearance at two Carnegie Hall charity concerts, also in 1963, was beset with behind-the-scenes rows over who should appear in which half of the shows. Sinatra eventually won the more important second half – then he refused Lena's suggestion they should get together to duet. Both concerts were a success – artistically and financially – but Horne refused to take a final bow with Sinatra.

At the beginning of the Seventies, Sinatra dropped a bombshell.

"I wish to announce, effective immediately, my retirement from the entertainment world and public life ..."

Thus began the official statement, issued on 21 March 1971, which stunned the world of entertainment. The proclamation went on to stress Sinatra's great fortune over three decades of activities which had been "fruitful, busy, uptight, loose, sometimes boisterous, occasionally sad, but always exciting ... "Apparently, there hadn't been too much opportunity for "reflection, reading, self-examination and that need which every thinking man has for a fallow period, a long muse in which to seek a better understanding of changes occurring in the world ... "

This, said the retiring Frank Sinatra, seemed to be a "proper time to take that breather".

It wasn't that people doubted that the "retirement" would last for long. It was the language used – it just didn't sound like Sinatra the Swinger. And even though the last 18 or so years had seen a relentless succession of professional undertakings and he was obviously feeling the cumulative effects, it never seemed that, at a premature 55, he could be gone from sight (and sound) forever ...

The "official" good-byes took the form of two farewell concerts (the same day) on 13 June and, in prescribed Sinatra style, at the 50th anniversary celebration of the Motion Picture & Television Relief Fund, on-stage at the Music Center, Los Angeles.

Tickets sold at a cool 250 bucks apiece. The supporting cast included Barbra Streisand, Pearl Bailey, Sammy Davis Jr, Rock Hudson, Jack Lemmon, the Fifth Dimension and Don Rickles.

The first of the concerts took place at the Dorothy Chandler Pavilion. It lasted for half-an-hour. The second, at the Ahmanson Theater, and also conducted by Nelson Riddle, ran for an additional 10 minutes. Both concerts ended, with – what else but? – "Angel Eyes", the archetypal Sinatra saloon song.

By all accounts, it was difficult to judge who was the most moved by the final " ... s'cuse me, while I disappear ... " – the singer or his rapt audience. Then, he was gone.

After this, the only times the Sinatra voice was now heard in public – featuring a small handful of songs on each occasion – occurred at political rallies on behalf of Spiro Agnew and Richard Nixon, during 1972.

By the end of the year, it seemed that Francis Albert still preferred retirement. And that's where he was gonna stay ...

1961-1972

RECORDS

ALTHOUGH SINATRA'S vast output of the Sixties might not always have matched the standards of the previous decade, there is no doubt that he produced a wider variety of work.

Being boss of your own company has obvious advantages and it gave Sinatra opportunities to record with legendary big bands, new writers and a selection of composers. During the second half of the decade, he even made an effort to come to grips with rock – though very much of the MOR variety, it must be said.

Of the first six albums completed for Reprise, four had newcomers on arranging/conducting duties. Album One, *Ring-a-Ding Ding!*, was the most overtly jazz-based set in the Sinatra discography so far.

One of the finest jazz writers to merge from the Fifties, Johnny Mandel came up with a series of first-class charts and *Ring-a-Ding Ding!* provided ample evidence of Sinatra's all-round ability to swing with undiminished power and elegance. New songs included "You And The Night And The Music", "Easy To Love", "In The Still Of The Night" and "A Fine Romance".

Sinatra Swings brought back the well-proven talents of Billy May and was a generally solid album, although, rhythmically, the singing lacked some of the crispness and spontaneity of the past.

There was little wrong, however, with a "Falling In Love With Love" and "Have You Met Miss Jones?". Best of all though was a two-and-a-half-chorus "You're Nobody 'Til Somebody Loves You", which remains one of Sinatra's most emphatically-swinging performances on record.

For his third album on Reprise, *I Remember Tommy,* Sinatra looked back to the band-singing days with Tommy Dorsey. It was thus a natural move to utilize the admirable services of Melvin "Sy" Oliver, a major contributor to Dorsey's output from 1939 to 1945.

Sinatra sung and swung with renewed vigour and thankfully the album wasn't just a pointless down-Memory-Lane excursion. In fact, there was very little attempt to replicate identically the original versions of the dozen numbers. "Without A Song", for example, was transformed in masterful fashion into a Basie-like swinger. So were the once plaintive "I'll Be Seeing You", the gentle "Imagination" and the restrained "East Of The Sun". A nice bonus was the vocal duet between Sinatra and his arranger-conductor on a crisply-swung "The One I Love".

Sinatra's fourth album for his own label was all-ballad, and *Sinatra & Strings* remains one of his finest albums. There is a passion and intensity – complemented, at times, with tenderness – that gives each performance a compelling quality. A rough edge to the voice gives added depth to such items as "I Hadn't Anyone Till You", "Don't Take Your Love From Me" and "Prisoner Of Love". "Night And Day", for so long associated with Sinatra, received its most expressive reading ever – the delivery of the verse is pure musical onomatopoeia.

The arrangements on *Sinatra & Strings* rank with any comparable backgrounds he worked with. These were the creations of Don Costa, the third newcomer on the list of Sinatra's writers in the early Sixties.

Arranger Gordon Jenkins was recalled for Album Number Five, which was also string-based. But *All Alone* failed to hit the mark, mainly because of its poor choice of repertoire. There was one superb piece of Sinatra-Jenkins, an achingly sad version of Irving Berlin's autobiographical "When I Lost You".

Further movement among Sinatra's arrangers found Neal Hefti scoring *Sinatra & Swingin' Brass*, which was, if anything, more jazz-oriented than *Ring-a-Ding Ding!* This time, there was a total absence of strings. And Hefti's charts never failed to swing, though the album is maybe a little busy in places (viz. "Pick Yourself Up", with its contrapuntal passages).

For the most part, there is much to appreciate in the singing. Especially, on "Don'cha Go 'Way Mad", (Porter's) "I Love You", "Tangerine", "I'm Beginning To See The Light" and "Serenade In Blue" (the sole ballad).

Writer Number Seven, Robert Farnon, wielded the baton to his own string-based arrangements as Musical Director for the disappointing *Great Songs From Great Britain*.

There was much *brouhaha* from Reprise's HQ in breaking the news that Frank Sinatra would be making his first-ever recordings with the Count Basie Orchestra. After all, a meeting between the Chairman of the Board (as WNEW disc jockey William B Williams had dubbed Sinatra) and the legendary jazz big band represented a summit meeting of two giant talents of the music world.

The resultant album – *Sinatra-Basie* - never fully lived up to its billing. On the positive side, the Rolls-Royce of post-war jazz orchestras provided the most lasting moment of *Sinatra-Basie* – a glorious utterly inimitable chorus on "I Won't Dance". Sinatra ("I've waited 20 years for this ... ") was, understandably, in awe of the band. It shows, too, for most of the album. He rarely sounded relaxed and the necessity of being locked into the band's fundamental 4/4 time signature seems to have been a problem.

A follow up studio collaboration didn't materialize until two-and-a-half years later. It was even less successful than the first. For one thing, *It Might As Well Be Swing* was a misleading description of the album's contents. Quincy Jones was in charge of arrangements and, frankly, they do not rank with that great man's finest. However, in two selections – "Fly Me To The Moon" and "The Best Is Yet To Come" – Sinatra, Jones and the band coalesce splendidly and show what might have been. They are the only memorable fruits of a thoroughly disappointing venture.

During the second half of the Sixties, Frank Sinatra and Count Basie worked together live on a fairly regular basis. Their third – and final – get-together on vinyl was the recording of a live performance for *Sinatra At The Sands*. Taped over several nights of their joint appearance at the Sands Hotel between 26 January and 1 February 1966, it was not only the best of their on-record collaborations, but represented the first time that Sinatra would release a live album – a two-LP set.

Sinatra's next studio album was a long-overdue reunion with arranger Nelson Riddle – except for a couple of singles dates, the first time they'd worked together for Reprise.

Perhaps though the concept of *The Concert Sinatra* was rather overblown. After all, did Sinatra really need Riddle to conduct an orchestra of over 60 pieces? Nevertheless, the results of this new undertaking were mostly fine. Only "Lost In The Stars" drew a less-than-convincing reading from the singer. Elsewhere, there were full-blooded versions of "Ol' Man River", "You'll Never Walk Alone" and "This Nearly Was Mine", plus an impassioned, superbly-sustained "Soliloquy" (from *Carousel*). Even better, though, were first-time recordings of "I Have Dreamed" and "My Heart Stood Still".

Nelson Riddle also worked on *Sinatra's Sinatra*, which

comprised reworkings of eleven Sinatra standards. The album offered evidence that perhaps it's best to leave the past to the past: not one of the new versions can be said to offer an improvement on previous recordings.

Riddle's last truly superb charts for entire Sinatra albums came with *Days Of Wine And Roses* (1964) and *Moonlight Sinatra* (1965). On the former set, the quartet of rhythm numbers easily came off best. Sinatra's timing on Crosby's "Swinging On A Star" was perfect. "The Way You Look Tonight", "In The Cool, Cool, Cool Of The Evening", "Days Of Wine And Roses" and "The Continental" were also successes. The ballads were not altogether well chosen, however. Both "It Might As Well Be Spring" and "Three Coins In The Fountain" were, like the new "Moon River", acceptable; but "Secret Love" remained very much the property of Doris Day; and "Love Is A Many-Splendored Thing" was, ultimately, The Four Aces', not Sinatra's. The all-ballad *Moonlight Sinatra* proved average-only fare.

The final Sinatra/Riddle collaboration of the decade, *Strangers In The Night* was a rush-job, a hotch-potch collection of oldies and newer things. Sinatra's reluctance to be hustled into the studio for a new album is shown by the unconvincing vocals on "My Baby Just Cares For Me", "You're Driving Me Crazy", "Call Me" and "Downtown". The only track that deserves any kind of praise was "Summer Wind", a superior Johnny Mercer ballad-with-a-lilting-swing.

After years of trying, Warners finally succeeded in their efforts to hoist Sinatra's name high among the biggest-selling rock artists. But, along the way, Sinatra was given an abundance of wretched material to record. *Cycles*, the album, was in many ways typical of the hotch-potch collections that were released during the mid-Sixties.

Its delightful, folksy title tune became a modest hit in the US. "Little Green Apples", a charming, if perhaps naive-sounding Bobby Russell piece, likewise made *Cycles* a better-than-average "modern" Sinatra album. The pièce de resistance, here, though, was the finest of all the numerous recordings of "By The Time I Get To Phoenix". Phrasing in classic style and sublime in his lyric-reading, Sinatra gave an undramatic, yet deeply-felt interpretation which the Jim Webb masterpiece would never receive elsewhere.

Don Costa produced a series of beautifully-sculpted charts for *A Man Alone* (1968), the album of Rod McKuen songs (and poems). And it was mostly the quiet understatement, vocally and instrumentally, which raised *A Man Alone* to a status of a real classic-ballad Sinatra collection, epitomized by individual tracks such as "Lonesome Cities", "I've Been To Town", "A Man Alone" and the wry "Love's Been Good To Me" (a major hit single in the UK).

Don Costa's arranging talents also contributed to *My Way*. As an album, it remains indicative of the erratic quality of some of Sinatra's offerings during this period. Worst of all was the brutal treatment meted out to Paul Simon's delightful, subtle and gentle "Mrs Robinson". Sadly, Costa takes a large share of the blame, with a sledgehammer arrangement that endeavoured to be a kind of big-band-Basie bash. Sinatra has a ball, it's true, but at the expense of the humour and content of the song's lyric. His substitution of "Jilly" for "Jesus" and the addition of "Keep those cards and letters comin' in, baby!" as a spoken coda were both tasteless and inappropriate.

The two Sinatra albums of the latter half of the Sixties which rightly have been acknowledged as masterpieces were the autobiographical *September Of My Years* (1965) and *Francis Albert Sinatra & Antonio Carlos Jobim* (1969).

Those who worked closely with Sinatra on the first-named have spoken with real pride of their involvement in the project. A project which dealt – unashamedly, tenderly, wistfully and sometimes humorously – with the subject of impending middle age. For Sinatra, it was the right time to make such a recorded statement – after all, he would be celebrating his 50th birthday at the year's end.

Sinatra himself was elated at the results. He must have known, for instance, that his reworkings of "Hello, Young Lovers" and "September Song" were considerable improvements on all previous versions. Even if, technically speaking, "Last Night When We Were Young" could not hope to surpass the recording on Capitol, it was nevertheless sung with supreme skill and know-how.

The first Sinatra/Jobim set comprised a septet of some of the choicest compositions by the celebrated Brazilian, who also played guitar, joining in on the vocal during several titles. Sinatra handled the English lyrics to such jewels as "The Girl From Ipanema", "Meditation", "How Insensitive" and "Quiet Nights Of Quiet Stars" with consummate skill. On standards such as "Change Partners", "I Concentrate On You" and "Baubles, Bangles And Beads", his phrasing was breathtaking.

Central to the triumphs of *September* and *Sinatra-Jobim* was the singer's unforced depth of expression. On *September*, there was genuine poignancy in his readings of the lyrics, and the series of ten performances he produced for the latter were suffused with a warmth and tenderness which compared favourably with any of his other recordings, no matter what era. As Sinatra himself would say later, he hadn't sung as softly in twenty years.

Two other Sixties albums which were, rightly, given the full promotional treatment were *Sinatra: A Man And His Music* (1965), a two-LP anthology looking back over his career in music and yet another collaboration between musical legends, *Francis A & Edward K.. Watertown* (1969) was another matter – a concept album in a basically "contemporary" mould, it was a commercial failure and an artistic success in part alone.

The retrospective *A Man & His Music* used recent recordings of pre-Reprise favourites, plus already-released material on that label, along with newly-created versions of "I'll Never Smile Again" and "Come Fly With Me".

The one-off collaboration with Ellington took place in 1967, *Francis A and Edward K*, didn't quite elicit the kind of magical results so many, including the two leading participants, had hoped for. Sinatra never sings poorly, yet here he didn't sound as inspired as working with Duke Ellington should have occasioned.

The first post-retirement album – *Sinatra & Company* – rescued all but two of the second Sinatra-Jobim get-together. (The remaining two tracks – "Bonita" and "Song Of The Sabia" – would remain unissued until included in a mid-Seventies British two-LP reissue compilation *Portrait Of Sinatra*.) Without equalling the flawless singing on the first LP, there was no doubt

that, once again, Sinatra and his Brazilian friend were completely *en rapport*. "Someone To Light Up My Life" and "This Happy Madness" were the pick of the bunch, together with "Wave", which included what surely must be Frank's lowest-ever note on record: going down with ease to E-flat.

Duke Ellington and Sinatra had a one-off recording date in 1969.

MOVIES

THE DECADE started more or less how the Fifties ended with two major movies in 1960 – *Can-Can* and *Some Came Running* – and a cameo role in *Pepe*. Over the next 10 years, there were to be further guest appearances in *The Road To Hong Kong* (1962), *The List Of Adrian Messenger* (1963), *The Oscar* (1966) and *Cast A Giant Shadow* (1966).

Sadly, in the Sixties, the non-stop series of films starring Sinatra was largely disappointing. Sinatra's continued involvement with the Clan (now more often called the Rat Pack) scarcely added to the overall quality of his movies, except for the entertaining *Robin And The 7 Hoods* (1964), a modern day version of the Robin Hood story set in Chicago gangland with a Cahn-Van Heusen score. Otherwise, there were turkeys such as *Sergeants 3* (1962), *4 For Texas* (1964) and *Marriage On The Rocks* (1965). Even these, however, were masterly by comparison with the forgettable, tasteless *Dirty Dingus Magee* (1969).

Background: Robin And The 7 Hoods; Below: The Manchurian Candidate.

Two more successful Sixties movies were *The Devil At Four O'Clock* (1961) and *None But The Brave* (1965), which marked Sinatra's directorial debut. In *Come Blow Your Horn* (1963), Sinatra again showed a deft comic touch alongside a bevy of glamorous "gals" and, in *The Naked Runner* (1967), Sinatra turned in a good performance as a businessman inveigled into killing a defected British spy.

By far the most important of Sinatra's Sixties films was *The Manchurian Candidate* (1962). Richard Condon's novel, about the brainwashing of a group of captured GIs in Korea, provided Hollywood with subject matter which it had never previously explored so deeply, or so cleverly. Sinatra's Captain Ben Marco is just about perfect, his portrayal both believable and sensitive.

Von Ryan's Express (1965) was one of those entertaining films turned out by Hollywood since the Fifties. Sinatra plays Colonel Joseph L Ryan, the lone Yank among a bunch of British POWs interned at an Italian war camp in 1943. The film's real star, though, was a magnificent old German steam engine.

Assault On A Queen (1966) involved a highly improbable attempt to hijack the liner *Queen Mary* using a reconditioned German U-boat and, in *The Detective* (1968), Sinatra played a dedicated cop. Of the remaining Swinging Sixties productions, there is little to choose between *Tony Rome* (1967) or its companion piece, *Lady In Cement* (1968). Both are taut, well-produced thrillers, with strong supporting casts.

GIGS

The most important performances by Frank Sinatra in the Sixties were the 30 dates
he played all over the world in aid of charity between April and June 1962.

There was no symphony-size orchestra this time – after all, Sinatra was paying the costs – but a solid sextet. Whether playing concerts in Mexico City, Tokyo, the Middle East or in Europe (Paris, London, Milan, Rome, Madrid, Athens, Monte Carlo), there was no doubting the overwhelming success of the tour. Not only were prodigious sums of money raised for charity, but the star's performances netted rave reviews everywhere.

Throughout the tour, Sinatra sounded buoyant. Just occasionally, tiredness prevented optimum delivery – as in one of the Tokyo concerts, where a revived "Moon Was Yellow" gave him some trouble, technically speaking. But at the Paris Lido, for example, on June 5, there were no problems [*Sinatra – The Paris Concert 1962*].

Sinatra's two admirable Paris concerts were preceded by four equally successful appearances across the Channel in London. As exhilarating as these performances were, the English capital was going to have to wait a further eight years before welcoming Sinatra back. Once again the Festival Hall was the venue for four charity concerts which illuminated the local music scene on consecutive nights (7 and 8 May) in 1970.

There are many who were present at these concerts who remain convinced that Frank Sinatra can never have sung better at any time during his career. (This writer is one.) As magnificent as his 1962 concerts had been, the two May 1970 concerts were truly something else.

It was the ballads that would really sign, seal and deliver his omnipotence on both evenings. There were nine ballads, first night; 10, the next. Each one was delivered with awesome technical ease and injected with a depth of expression that was astonishing.

Come Fly with Frank! Sinatra charms the citizens of Tokyo during his world charity tour in 1962.

These particular versions of "Autumn Leaves", using the classic Jenkins arrangement, eclipsed even the 1962 interpretation in the same hall. It was the first ballad on both evenings – and almost at once, it seemed, Sinatra had deserted the joyful ambience of the swingers for an atmosphere of near-despair and sadness. This feeling was sustained by what were surely the finest live readings of "Yesterday" by any singer. The most incredible single performance, on both evenings, was "Ol' Man River". Knowledgeable Sinatra connoisseurs remember them as his most technically accomplished interpretations and, just as important, probably the most emotionally charged.

Sinatra returned to the Festival Hall on 16 November to give two further high-calibre performances with an all-British orchestra. Both performances were introduced delightfully by Princess Grace of Monaco.

Concert tours with the big bands of Basie and Rich were also important events in the Sinatra calendar of the Sixties. The decision to take a top-grade outfit on to the road proved to be of signal importance, especially in respect of outdoors live appearances. And the one event which crystallized the kind of future activities was the Newport Jazz Festival gig with Count Basie's orchestra, in July 1965. It indicated to Sinatra that he, too, could replicate what the big-name rock artists and bands were doing at open-air concerts, including oversized festivals like Woodstock and the Isle of Wight.

Both singer and band, conducted by Quincy Jones, were warmly received throughout their one-hour stint at Newport. The wide-ranging programme included "Get Me To The Church On Time", "Fly Me To The Moon", "Street Of Dreams", the crowd-pleasing "Luck Be A Lady", and "I've Got You Under My Skin". "Hello, Dolly" (hardly a jazz-purist choice, despite featuring Harry Edison on trumpet, as on the recording) was the low-point of the 18-number selection.

The major problem, musically speaking, came with the out-and-out ballads. The classic Basie four-in-the-bar rhythm was inappropriate for truly meaningful readings of classics like "In The Wee Small Hours Of The Morning", "It's Easy To Remember" and "Call Me Irresponsible".

By the Forest Hills concert, five days later, this problem was showing signs of being resolved. The Sinatra-Basie partnership grew into compatibility through regular collaboration. With the Buddy Rich Orchestra, by contrast, Sinatra seemed to strike an instant rapport. His five-gig stint with Rich in July 1967 – which opened in Cleveland and ended in Baltimore – found him in far better voice and obviously enjoying the excellent support. There were no rigid 4/4 restrictions with Rich – the swing numbers swung in a gloriously freewheeling way. And the ballads were performed in classic Sinatra style.

In 1971, Sinatra appeared for the farewell concerts in LA. This was not the wise-cracking Sinatra of yore. Obviously moved both by the occasion itself and the responsive presence of an all-star bill and a star-studded audience, he looked tense and at times close to tears. But ever the true professional, he turned in the kind of performances any self-respecting entertainer would hope for – particularly, it was reported, for the second concert.

He sang songs from every part of his career: "All Or Nothing At All", saluted the all-too-brief period with Harry James ... "I'll Never Smile Again" did the same for the Tommy Dorsey Orchestra. ... "Ol' Man River" took him back to MGM musicals and dozens of Sinatra bravura performances, live and on record ... "Try A Little Tenderness" and "Nancy" were redolent of the Forties; "The Lady Is A Tramp", "Angel Eyes" and "I've Got You Under My Skin" epitomized, in their different moods and ways, the triumphs of post-*Eternity* years ... "Fly Me To The Moon" recalled the happy, swinging years in front of the Basie band ... The personalised statements that were "That's Life" and "My Way" seemed to personify the whole Sinatra aura – songs to which only *he* had truly given meaning .

And it just had to be a genuine saloon song, "Angel Eyes", an enduring jewel in his bulging casket of diverse material, that would take him offstage, at both farewell events ...

Sinatra and Basie – the partnership got better and better.

TELEVISION

SINATRA'S TV activities during the Sixties were dominated by a five-show series under his own name which, at long last, would make him a legend of the small-screen.

Sinatra: A Man And His Music [*Frank Sinatra: A Man And His Music* (1965) on video] was the turning point. With a large orchestra in full view, this includes 17 well-chosen songs – five of which were woven skilfully into a satisfying medley, which was one of several peaks of excellence. And Sinatra is in full control, from the moment he seats himself calmly on a stool for a storming "I've Got You Under My Skin".

It would be difficult for *A Man And His Music, Part 2* – (1966), also on video – to replicate its predecessor's brilliance. Daughter Nancy duets with Dad on "Yes Sir, That's My Baby" and "Downtown". But it was the Ballad Medley which was the single highlight. Using "Just One Of Those Things" as the link song, it was beautifully realized and performed with supreme conviction.

The third in the series was something extra-special. So special, in fact, that *A Man & His Music + Ella + Jobim* – (1967), also on video – will probably never be surpassed. With Riddle wielding the baton, this was as near to being the perfect musical TV show as possible. Sinatra's joy at having Ella Fitzgerald as his principal guest showed in the way he actively encouraged her to perform in the most free-and-easy way – just like a kind of private jam session, instead of a well-structured media presentation. As exhilarating as the Frank-Ella duets were, for many viewers the absolute peak in this remarkable programme was reached when Sinatra, taking

vocal lead, and Jobim reproduced in miniature much of the magic of their recordings of "Quiet Nights", "Change Partners", "I Concentrate On You" and "The Girl From Ipanema".

Francis Albert Does His Thing in 1968, the fourth in a series of Sinatra shows.

The fourth show couldn't possibly hope to achieve the artistic heights of the previous year. *Francis Albert Does His Thing* – (1968), also on video – had Don Costa making his Sinatra/TV debut. It also had two guests – Diahann Carroll and the 5th Dimension.

The Ballad Medley in the fifth and last of the series proved to be a major disappointment. This was due to Sinatra suffering from some kind of laryngitic problem. Indeed, it affected practically every number he performed during the simply named *Sinatra* – (1969), also on video.

Surprise! Surprise! *Ol' Blue Eyes is back again ... !*

Sinatra – mega-star. His insatiable quest to sing before more and bigger audiences would dominate the rest of his career. The Living Legend goes on and on and ...

Around the time of the White House gig for Richard Nixon and Italian Premier Andreotti, rumours of a Sinatra comeback began to circulate.

Towards the end of April 1973, under a heavy cloak of secrecy and in the company of conductor Don Costa, Sinatra entered the Goldwyn Studios in Hollywood armed with two new songs, Kris Kristofferson's "Nobody Wins" and "Noah" by Joe Raposo. These numbers were almost certainly intended for a new LP – unfortunately, it was an unsuccessful session and the masters were destroyed.

Undeterred, Costa and Sinatra – this time joined by Gordon Jenkins – returned to the same studios several times before the end of August. The result was the first comeback album, consisting of a dozen numbers by contemporary writers, ranging from Raposo and Kristofferson to Stephen Sondheim and Paul and John Williams.

Its title, *Ol' Blue Eyes Is Back,* gave rise to the most popular Sinatra epithet since "The Voice" and it was also used for the singer's comeback TV special. Transmitted on 18 November 1973, the show offered living proof that he was indeed back, if perhaps a little overweight this time around. But the critics were mostly kind: as the *New York Daily News* put it, "We thought we were through writing love-letters to Frank Sinatra. Here we go again!" If 1973 was the Year Of The Comeback, the rest of the Seventies proved Sinatra was going to be around for a while. 1974 set the pattern with concerts at innumerable venues – from plush indoor night–spots and concert halls to huge outdoor arenas.

It was this insatiable quest to sing before more and bigger audiences which would dominate the rest of Sinatra's career. Unable to exist without adulation, the Living Legend was transforming himself into a modern superstar.

His first full comeback performance took place on 25 January 1974 at Caesar's Palace – his first booking there since 1968. In March, Sinatra embarked on a twelve-concert tour in aid of the Variety Clubs International.

In July, Sinatra returned to Australia on a brief tour that soon ran into problems. True to form, there were several altercations between the visitor and the local press, which included allegations by a cameraman that one of Sinatra's bodyguards had looped an electric flex around his neck. During the rapturously-received 75-minute performance which followed, Frank told the 8,000-strong Melbourne audience what he thought of Australian journalists,

"They are bums and parasites, who have never done an honest day's work. Most of them are a bunch of fags, anyway ..."

adding for good measure that the female variety were

"buck-and-a-half hookers".

As it turned out, this wasn't a smart move. After the Australian Journalists' Association had called upon fellow trades union affiliates to boycott him, Sinatra found there was no one to serve him food and drink, or to carry his baggage; moreover, he couldn't use any form of public transport to get him to the airport ... let alone find anyone to service his private jet.

Following negotiations, apologies came from both sides – as a goodwill gesture, Sinatra took no fee for the third of the Melbourne gigs, which was televised.

The Seventies were a decade of non-stop touring, at home and abroad. Back in the US, he appeared in court on charges of ordering his bodyguards to beat up a young insurance agent, Frank Weinstock, at a Palm Springs hotel.

Sinatra's relief at being found not guilty must have been tempered when Jilly Rizzo, his close friend and personal minder, was fined over $100,000 for assault and battery.

Following the case, it was off to Lake Tahoe, Nevada, for seven days at the plush Harrah's in September – and a first-time association with the marvellous Woody Herman band.

After a 24-hour break, the Sinatras quit Tahoe for seven days at Caesar's Palace and this was followed in October by a nation-wide tour – Woody Herman's splendid young orchestra provided the concerts with their own brand of big-band excitement. And he rounded off a truly energetic year with a memorable performance at the Diplomat, Miami, on New Year's Eve.

1975 saw no let-up in Sinatra's programme. The star played Caesar's Palace on no fewer than four occasions; he visited Europe twice; then, in November, he returned to London, before concerts in Iran and Israel. In all, Sinatra made a remarkable 140 individual performances in 105 days, appearing before audiences in excess of 500,000 at home and abroad.

During his European travels, Sinatra fell out with the German press, arousing much controversy in the process. In London, his rage undiminished, he lambasted German journalists on-stage at the Albert Hall for saying he was "a super-gangster and ... a pathetic alcoholic whose career is over". His torrid outburst went on: "I could have answered them and told reporters to look to the sins of their fathers. I could have mentioned Dachau. They are the gangsters ... "

Within the packed hall, where the audience included Princess Margaret, Princess Anne and Princess Grace of Monaco, a kind of stunned silence prevailed for the most part.

From a personal standpoint, the twelve London concerts of 1975 provided outstanding memories. Sinatra has never disguised his delight at the genuine warmth shown to him on his trips to Britain. Invariably – some might say uncannily – he has succeeded in singing at or near to his very best when performing in front of audiences there.

Following the twin triumphs of 1975, his appearances back in London in 1977 and 1978 were, if anything, even more enthusiastically received. And Sinatra himself responded in even finer voice too.

Throughout the Seventies, he shared the stage with a variety of top-grade talent including Ella Fitzgerald, Count Basie, Sarah Vaughan and John Denver. During 1977, Dean Martin and Sinatra worked together for the first time in years and, 12 months on, Sammy Davis Jr also worked briefly with his Rat Pack chief.

But by far the most unusual individual gig of the Seventies – geographically speaking – took place on 27 September 1979, when Sinatra performed in Egypt, against a backdrop of the Pyramids. The concert, in aid of a local children's charity, was described by Egyptian President Anwar Sadat as "an unforgettable experience".

The perfect end to the year, perhaps – and indeed the decade – came during his 64th birthday party at Caesar's Palace. Sinatra was visibly moved when presented with the prestigious Pied Piper Award by the American Society of Composers, Authors & Publishers.

For Sinatra, the saddest event of the decade was the death of his mother Dolly. She was travelling from Palm Springs to Las Vegas for the opening night of her son's latest Caesar's Palace engagement, when the Lear jet in which she was a passenger hit a mountain-side. After playing the opening two shows, Frank cancelled the rest of the season. Dolly's death was confirmed, four days later, when her body was recovered from a snow-covered ridge. The funeral took place on 13 January 1977.

Other deaths which caused Sinatra great sadness during the Seventies were those of his mentor Bing Crosby and Hank Sanicola, his former song publisher, plugger and friend. An altogether happier event was his marriage in July 1976 to Barbara Marx, formerly married to Zeppo Marx.

In 1980, he received the Johnny Mercer Award for his "lifetime romance with the American Songwriter" as well as a special Humanitarian Award, for his untiring efforts to raise money for needy and handicapped children. From then on, the number of awards, accolades and presentations would continue to increase.

And his singing still made people happy – the 1980 London concerts were a good example. Sinatra appeared, in consecutive week-long stints at the Festival and Albert Halls. At both venues, he performed with undiminished brilliance. And any thoughts that, approaching 65, his appeal must have waned were dispelled by the avalanche of letters requesting tickets.

1981 began with a lengthy application by Sinatra to obtain a licence as public relations and entertainment consultant for his second home – Caesar's Palace. (The alleged Sinatra-Mafia link came up again in *The Last Mafioso*, a book based on the confessions of Jimmy "The Weasel" Fratianno, a Mafia hit-man, who claimed that Frank had been front-man, acting for Chicago mobsters, in respect of the ownership of a gambling casino at Lake Tahoe, Nevada.)

In February, he testified before the Gaming Control Commission, who returned the gaming licence that had been taken away almost 20 years before. President Reagan gave a personal reference, describing Sinatra as "an honourable person".

In July, Frank made his first ever trip to Sun City in *apartheid*-bound South Africa and insisted on playing to non-segregated audiences.

The following January, at Radio City Music Hall, Sinatra and Luciano Pavarotti performed together for the first time. And, once again, Sinatra appeared before a huge audience in the Dominican Republic [*Concert For The Americas,* available on video] accompanied by the Buddy Rich Orchestra. During 1982, he also appeared alongside Nancy Reagan, singing "To Love A Child" on the South Lawn of the White House to promote Mrs Reagan's book about foster-parents.

Within a five-month period in 1983, two of Sinatra's closest and most important musical associates died. Don Costa on 19 January;

and Gordon Jenkins on 1 May. It was fitting that both these great talents should have contributed significantly to *She Shot Me Down* (1981), the last Sinatra album of genuine quality.

On a happier note, 1983 closed with an all-star party thrown by the Variety Club. Richard Burton delivered a glowing oral tribute. Calling him "a giant", Burton said of Sinatra:

> # *"Other than himself, there is no one who knows the magnitude of his generosity."*

Record-wise, 1984 should have provided one album at least that would satisfy both his long-time followers and younger admirers. Even at the age of 68, a Sinatra-Quincy Jones album seemed a perfect way of reviving his recording career. Unfortunately, *LA Is My Lady* (1984) seemed to indicate that, in the area of recording at least, Sinatra should finally close the book.

During the remainder of the Eighties, he continued to strut his stuff on stage but there were worries about his health. In November 1986, surgeons performed an emergency operation to remove an abscess from his large intestine. Two months later, he underwent further surgery. But a third operation, in early February 1987, was less serious – doctors explained it was to remove scar tissue from the previous surgery. Not long after, the redoubtable Sinatra re-commenced gigging.

By June 1988, he had undertaken an Italian concert tour. Three months later, he gave eight performances at Carnegie Hall, with 74-year-old jazz giant, Lionel Hampton, in support.

In December, at a huge press conference, Sinatra, Dean Martin and Sammy Davis Jr gave the news of an impending 29-city tour, titled Together Again. The American Express-sponsored tour commenced on March 13 and continued until the 20th, when Martin bowed out.

Sinatra and Davis played a further seven dates in tandem, before Martin's replacement, Liza Minnelli, made it three again.

The new all-star package called itself The Ultimate Event. For most of 1990, Sinatra's activities would revolve around The Ultimate Event with a further tour of the US and Europe. The caravan continued rolling until the middle of the year when an ailing Sammy Davis quit. On 16 May 1990, he died in LA at the age of 64.

In 1990, two further deaths affected Sinatra. In January he lost long-time friend Harold Arlen, one of the greatest of all pop-music composers. And less than a month later, his very close buddy, songwriter Jimmy Van Heusen, passed on too.

By the end of the year, one thing was certain: it had *not* been a very good year. And there were more grievous losses to come ...

However, neither Sinatra's periods of hospitalization nor the deaths of those close to him could coax the superstar back into retirement – a genuine, no-going-back retirement, this time.

Even so, a growing number of people were beginning to believe – privately and otherwise – that as of now, or very shortly, it really was time for Frank Sinatra to quit. And the reasons were becoming all too obvious, and increasingly so . . .

Doin' it their way – Frank and Sammy get their instructions from Liza during one of the hugely successful Ultimate Events.

RETROSPECTIVES

1973-1989

RECORDS

In the 11 years following his return to full-time singing, Frank Sinatra cut just half-a-dozen albums: unfortunately, over 60 different recording sessions between April 1973 and June 1988 produced remarkably few items suitable for release.

Ol' Blue Eyes Is Back (1973), however, was as good a comeback album as anyone could have wished for. It featured an intriguing variety of fresh material, including the poignant and unusual "There Used To Be A Ballpark", the celebratory "You Will Be My Music" and, of course, "Send In The Clowns".

The follow-up LP, *Some Nice Things I've Missed* (1974), certainly had its moments, although you couldn't number "Tie A Yellow Ribbon" and Neil Diamond's "Sweet Caroline" among those.

The prospect of a live album with the superb Woody Herman Orchestra in sterling support was mouth-watering. Unfortunately, *The Main Event* (1974) proved to be the first real dud of the post-retirement period. Purported to have been recorded at Madison Square Garden on 13 October, the contents were, in fact, pilfered from five different concerts – including Madison Square – between October 2 and 13. It was the kind of dishonesty which record companies have been guilty of for many years but it was still a shame that overall the singing did not match the tremendous support from Herman & Co.

As Sinatra grew older, recordings were all too often aborted and hits grew scarce. In 1974, there was a short-lived chart life in Britain for "I Believe I'm Gonna Love You", which peaked at Number 34, during a low-key, seven-week chart stay.

Six years later, a new Sinatra album was released, a triple-LP set. Titled *Trilogy*, it was conceived in three parts – *Past* (with Billy May arrangements), *Present* (Don Costa, Nelson Riddle) and *Future* (Gordon Jenkins).

Past was the best of the three. Though scarcely vintage Sinatra, it wasn't at all bad. *Present* was less successful. The third part of *Trilogy* is the one which continues to cause the most arguments. Indeed, it remains the most controversial of any Sinatra record project. Brilliantly written and conceived as it was, there remains an overall aura of sycophancy, combined with pretentiousness, which proved indigestible for many listeners.

Swingin' with Quince – Sinatra acknowledges a long-time musical associate, Quincy Jones.

In fact, by far the best Seventies/Eighties album was *She Shot Me Down* (1981). Its completion at five different dates, over a period of six months, mirrored Sinatra's erratic recording pattern of the time. Material-wise, it was the most intriguing album since, say, *Cycles*. Mostly, it was comprised of new songs, by Jule Styne, with Susan Birkenhead ("Hey Look, No Crying"), Stephen Sondheim ("Good Thing Going"), Pamela Phillips and Don Costa ("Monday Morning Quarterback"), Gordon Jenkins ("I Loved Her"), and Alec Wilder & Loonis McGlohan ("South – To A Warmer Place"). Not all the singing was vintage Sinatra, but he read both the old and the "modern" lyrics with an understanding and technical control that was often lacking in his later recordings.

In his 69th year, Sinatra once again collaborated with Quincy Jones – and he could scarcely have hoped for better sidemen on *LA Is My Lady* . Unfortunately, his voice was not at its best during the three sessions needed to complete the LP. *LA Is My Lady* was released together with a single, the pedestrian "Until The Real Thing Comes Along", in 1980, but the latter failed to take off in any territory.

Sinatra's recording activities for the decade ended there. (Two special Sinatra collections were released to celebrate his 75th birthday in 1990. Capitol/EMI put together a commemorative three-CD/five-LP box [*The Capitol Years*]. Warner's, not to be outdone, produced its own 81-track, four-CD/six-LP box set – [*The Reprise Collection*]. Both were excellent in concept and production.)

If Sinatra's record output during the later period produced very little substantial product, it did at least create another kind of record when "Theme From New York, New York" became a modest hit in 1980. This meant that Sinatra had equalled the almost unbelievable feat of Louis Armstrong (1926-66) of 40 years in the *Billboard* singles charts. Sinatra's feat had begun with Tommy Dorsey's recording of "Polka Dots And Moonbeams" in 1940 and came full-circle with "New York, New York".

His involvement with recording fading fast, concerts would inevitably come to dominate Sinatra's time in the Eighties.

GIGS

The gruelling schedule kept up by Sinatra throughout the Seventies, and for most of the following decade, might have taxed the resources of a man half his age, but he was determined to remain at the top.

After nearly a year of preparation, Sinatra staged his first major comeback performance in January 1974 with his return to Caesar's Palace. Looking fit and healthy, he sang with renewed vigour and much of his pre-retirement magic intact. Even the cancellation of a couple of shows, due to throat problems, couldn't detract from a triumphant return.

On 8 April, with Bill Miller conducting, Sinatra made his long-awaited debut at Carnegie Hall, with a well-chosen mix of songs old and new. Soon he was flying off to Japan and Australia: Sinatra took Tokyo by storm, following up his success with a 35-minute show for US service personnel on board the *USS Midway*, moored at the Yokosuka Naval base.

Later that year, came eight days at the plush Harrah's, Lake Tahoe, which found Sinatra sharing the spotlight with Frank Jr and Nancy Jr – as well as Woody Herman's "Young Thundering Herd".

The Vegas gigs were a prelude to Sinatra touring with the Herman band for almost a month. Starting in Boston and finishing in Dallas, the itinerary included two outdoor gigs at New York's Madison Square Garden. Although the tour produced much fine music, there were times when the strain of such a punishing schedule showed through and Sinatra sounded tired.

1975 saw further extensive touring. There were superlative performances on two consecutive nights in London (29/30 May) at what the singer had re-titled the "Francis Albert Hall".

On the opening night, Sinatra sang with extraordinary power throughout an 80-minute performance, which included Stevie Wonder's "You Are The Sunshine Of My Life", "My Way", "I See Your Face Before Me', "Last Night When We Were Young", "Cycles", "Strangers In The Night" and, a delightful revival from almost 30 years before, "But Beautiful".

Perhaps the highlight of the year found Sinatra playing two weeks at the famous Uris Theatre in New York in September, joined by Ella Fitzgerald and the Count Basie Orchestra. Ella and Basie took care of the first half. Sinatra, with Basie, closed. At the end of his performance, Frank invited Ella back on-stage, for a series of joyous duets.

As the touring wound on relentlessly during the remainder of the Seventies, Sinatra started playing venues he'd almost certainly never worked before (e.g. Tarrytown, New York and the brand new, 3,500-seater Westchester Premier Theatre). This unremitting schedule went on into the next decade.

And what better way to start a new decade than by getting your name into the *Guinness Book Of Records*? That's what happened following Frank's first-ever appearance in Rio de Janeiro's vast Maracana Stadium on 26 January 1980. An awesome 175,000 crowd gave him the kind of welcome which, according to one of the musical entourage, "shook us all to the foundations – Frank himself was staggered by the sheer volume of the applause that greeted his arrival on-stage". Sinatra repaid his record audience with an 18-number performance that few of them would ever forget.

Sinatra was equally generous in the size of his programme for his return to Carnegie Hall five months later, where a capacity audience roared its approval at yet another enactment of artistry proving that, in his 65th year, he had taken on a new lease of life.

By September 1984, however, there were telltale signs of deterioration in his vocal output during the Albert Hall concerts: the personality of the man was beginning to be of real importance in getting him through the more technically taxing ballads.

Nonetheless, in September 1985, Sinatra appeared in Milan for a lengthy concert appearance that silenced anyone thinking he was over the hill. Forget lack of staying power, the second part of an 80-minute stint turned out better than the first!

The Ultimate Event package tours took up a lot of Frank's time during 1988-90. Originally, the idea was for Sinatra, Sammy Davis Jr and Dean Martin to perform under a Together Again banner. Each would undertake his own set, with all three stars appearing together for the final section of each concert.

But the Sinatra-Martin-Davis triumvirate lasted only as far as Chicago. On Sinatra's strong advice, it was reported, Martin quit. His performances had been consistently erratic – and some concert-goers had complained that he'd talked more than sung during his contributions.

Sinatra and Davis continued the tour in Cincinnati as a duo, before Liza Minnelli was asked to join them – and the package was retitled The Ultimate Event. They were to prove a winning team, embarking on a mini world tour in 1988 and continuing intermittently up to late March 1990, when Sammy Davis had to leave.

The personality of the man began to be of real importance in ballads.

TELEVISION

After his comeback in 1973, there were no more TV series in Frank Sinatra's name but he did make numerous guest appearances on other peoples' shows.

The one-off, *Ol' Blue Eyes Is Back* was just the kind of small-screen presentation he needed to advertise his return. Following a sequence of excerpts from his movies, Sinatra and Gene Kelly duetted with charm. The acid test, though, was the classic Ballad Medley. While in no way equalling the superlative medleys from the *Man & His Music* series, quality permeated the readings of "Last Night When We Were Young", "Violets For Your Furs" and "Here's That Rainy Day". [All featured on the video, *Ol' Blue Eyes Is Back*].

The Main Event (1974, available on video) was very much a *live* performance. Taped at Madison Square Garden, *The Main Event* was recorded as part of a tour, which might explain why The Voice was hoarse and rough-edged in places. The ballads, in particular, suffered – "The House I Live In", the penultimate number, came off worst. The audience, though, were over the moon.

Predictably, *Frank Sinatra & Friends* (1977, available on video) proved to be a form of mutual admiration society. After they had contributed one number apiece on their own, Friends – like Dean Martin, Tony Bennett, Natalie Cole – engaged Sinatra in duets. More important than these, of course, were Sinatra's own solo efforts, including a hard-swinging "Where Or When", an expressive "Night And Day" and a dull-thud average "Everybody Ought To Be In Love".

Sinatra: The First 40 Years (1980, available on video) was, not surprisingly, cast in a similar mould. Taped at Caesar's Palace on his 64th birthday, the recipient sat in kingly fashion – front row – with wife Barbara and daughters Nancy and Tina in attendance as a bevy of headliners ventured on stage to pay their respects. Naturally, the hero of the hour needed little persuading to take his rightful place on-stage to close the evening's proceedings.

Television became less and less important to Sinatra as the Eighties wore on. Perhaps his personal highlight came in 1988 with his two-song salute in *The Tribute To Irving Berlin* show: Sinatra sang "When I Lost You" and "Remember" much to the joy of a crowded Carnegie Hall.

The huge global success of The Ultimate Event was also celebrated on video (*Frank, Liza And Sammy: The Ultimate Event*) with contributions from all three participants.

Ol' Blue Eyes is Back – here with his ol' buddy, Gene Kelly – in the TV show of that name.

Acting-wise, Sinatra's only small screen appearance of the Eighties came 10 years after *Contract On Cherry* (1977), when the singer played a tough ex-cop in an episode of *Magnum*.

No One more for the Road

The spirit is willing, but . . . Here's Sinatra, in concert, in Richmond, VA., March 1994, where he collapsed from exhaustion.

The announcement came at the beginning of December 1994: Following a double-concert at the Fukuoko Dome, Tokyo, later that month, Frank Sinatra would be ceasing live performance for ever to concentrate on recording.

Media reaction to this news was curiously muted, perhaps because the decision came as no surprise to those who had been following Sinatra's career.

Years of remorseless touring had taken their toll. Probably the saddest indication of Sinatra's declining powers was the regular presence on-stage of a lyric-prompter, helping the greatest interpreter of the popular lyric to remember his lines even on unforgettable classics such as "They Can't Take That Away From Me" and "My Kind Of Town", songs Sinatra had long since made his own.

Despite being in his seventies, Sinatra kept pushing himself to the limits. In 1990 and 1991, he toured with husband and wife duo Steve Lawrence and Eydie Gorme and played well received concerts in Australia, Norway and Ireland. There was also a brief professional reunion with Shirley MacLaine – but they parted on bad terms.

The following year, Sinatra returned to London, where once again he wowed his audiences. The only major disappointment was the opening night, when the venerable Sinatra showed obvious signs of distraction and provided the author (and others) with first-hand evidence of the debilitating effects of old age: the veteran superstar misread the lyrics of half-a-dozen numbers, as well as re-entering two bars early for an otherwise acceptable "Moonlight In Vermont".

1993 saw no let-up in Sinatra's crowded schedule, which included concerts in Sweden and Germany as well as the usual hectic itinerary in the United States. By this time, however, there had been a sea change in the press's attitude towards the singer. Journalists no longer came to bury Sinatra, but to offer sympathetic praise.

There were particularly joyful reactions to a triumphant five-show stint at the Sands Hotel in Atlantic City in November 1993, as well as the Foxwoods Resort and Casino a year later. However, at

Richmond in March 1994, Sinatra collapsed at a Sunday evening concert while singing "My Way".

In the Nineties all thoughts of a new record were put to one side until the middle of 1993, when Sinatra went back inside the studio at Capitol Tower to lay down his own contributions to a special album project called *Duets*.

Thanks to the marvels of modern technology, Sinatra was able to duet with the likes of Barbra Streisand, Tony Bennett, Carly Simon, Charles Aznavour, Aretha Franklin and Bono from U2 without actually being in the same studio at the same time with any of them. Indeed, some of his partners literally phoned their performances in – "digitally" – down the line. Sales in excess of 5 million world-wide guaranteed a *Duets II,* featuring Stevie Wonder and Gladys Knight among others.

These albums also inspired a CBS TV special, *Duets*, which arguably overshadowed the Golden Globe-winning mini-TV series, *Sinatra*, reputedly costing $18 million and described as a "candid portrayal" of the singer's life.

Bowing out gracefully after his double triumph in Tokyo in December 1994, Sinatra is now retired and it remains to be seen whether he will be making any more recordings. Or indeed comeback performances.

One thing is certain. There will never be anyone else like Hoboken's most famous son.

As Sinatra himself declared to the audience at the end of one of his Nineties concerts,

"May you live to 750 and may the last voice you hear be mine..."

Trust Francis Albert to write his own epitaph.

Selected A-Z Discography Videography and Filmography

Space considerations preclude full listings. The Discography and Videography, which covers all media, is fairly comprehensive and provides a listing of individual record and video titles, plus sources. Where possible, I have listed CD releases in preference to LPs (which are indicated thus – *). But where important vinyl albums have not been re-released in the compact disc format, LP information is given. Many Sinatra albums can be found – often at favourable cut-down prices – at specialist retail shops or record fairs.
The bold numbers ranged right indicate page references in this book.

Radio Recordings

FRANK SINATRA: LIVE 1943-46 (Jazz Hour). Further superior airshots. Most intriguing of all are three numbers ("Couldn't Sleep A Wink"; "Close To You"; "You'll Never Know") with typically gorgeous Stordahl orchestral arrangements which Sinatra would have used at his first (*a cappella*) recording dates for Columbia.

FRANK SINATRA: 1949 LITE-UP TIME SHOWS (Jazz Band) 23 performances from Sinatra's last radio series of the Forties-into-the-Fifties, with as varied a mixture as before (e.g. "You're The Cream In My Coffee"; "Body & Soul"; "All Of Me"). **73**

FRANK SINATRA: 1946 OLD GOLD SHOWS (Jazz Hour). Two complete Old Gold (2 January and 30 October 1946), with Peggy Lee guest-appearing on the first. Plus a half-dozen fine performances from other shows, including among the six undocumented numbers "What Am I Gonna Do About You?", a Cahn-Styne tune never recorded commercially by Sinatra or anybody else.

FRANK SINATRA: "THERE'LL BE SOME CHANGES MADE":

THE RARITIES 1950-51 (Voice). A 32-number selection of Sinatra's earliest own TV show performances – including duets with June Hutton and Skitch Henderson – which offers conclusive proof that, whatever his personal/professional problems at that time, he still sang with great skill and emotion.

FRANK SINATRA: "THE VOICE" 1943-1947 (Decade Records). Yet another fascinating collection of broadcast performances, including two complete shows from December 1943, plus some rare radio-rehearsal material from 1946.

FRANK SINATRA: YOUR HIT PARADE 1944: IT WAS A VERY GOOD YEAR (JRRecords). Skilfully-remastered, 19-number collection of material from some of Sinatra's most important radio series of the Forties, including the complete show of 23/12/44. **56, 73**

FRANK SINATRA: YOUR HIT PARADE 1947 (JRRecords) Average-to-good Sinatra fare. **73**

* GOT THE WORLD ON A STRING (Starburst) Twenty superb examples of Sinatra's finest radio series (*To Be Perfectly Frank*), including "Thou Swell", "Just You Just Me", "Where Or When", "Platinum Blues". **97**

HARRY JAMES & HIS ORCHESTRA: AMERICAN DANCES BROADCASTS * (Jasmine). Two complete broadcasts: the first – featuring two Sinatra numbers ("To You"; "From The Bottom Of My Heart"), linked with the BBC in London.

HARRY JAMES & HIS ORCHESTRA: BANDSTAND MEMORIES 1938 TO 1948 (Hindsight). Boxed set, containing 20-page booklet, with performances by several vocalists including Frank Sinatra (seven titles, of which three – "Wishing"; "If I Didn't Care"; "The Lamp Is Low" – he would never record commercially). **32, 37**

LIVE DUETS 1943-1957 (Voice). Duettists included pianist Skitch Henderson (medley of nine tunes), Dinah Shore, Dorothy Kirsten, Nat Cole, Margaret Whiting – all from radio; and Bing Crosby, Louis Armstrong – from TV shows. **73**

1935-1939 THE BEGINNING & HARRY JAMES (FS) Containing all known Sinatra-James recordings (including alternative takes for "From The Bottom Of My Heart"; "Here Comes The Night"; "All Or Nothing At All"), plus complete broadcast from the Roseland Ballroom (19/7/39); also two broadcasts featuring the Hoboken Four ("Shine"; "Curse Of An Aching Heart") and the demo disc, made privately by Sinatra, presumably to celebrate his wedding the following day, "Our Love". **22, 23, 32**

PERFECTLY FRANK: LIVE BROADCAST PERFORMANCES 1953-1955
(Bravura). A magnificent 31-track selection of the finest singing Sinatra produced on any radio series. Many of the songs (e.g. "You Took Advantage Of Me"; "I'm In The Mood For Love"; "Tenderly") were never recorded commercially by Sinatra. **118**

THE RAREST SINATRA [1937-46] (Decade Records)
Fascinating collection of broadcast material – including two TV items from 1951 and an absorbing New York-BBC link-up from 1944, with Sinatra singing "These Foolish Things" and "Come Out, Wherever You Are". Earliest item finds a non-singing Sinatra conducting (!) an awful Dixie combo the Four Sharps on Fred Allen's *Town Hall Tonight* show... rare, but understandably so... ?

SINATRA: PORTRAITS FROM THE PAST [1943-46] (Bravura)
Satisfying collection of radio material, a mixture of sings he never did elsewhere, including "I'll Walk Alone", "Three Little Words", "Ac-Cent-Tchu-Ate The Positive".

SINATRA: THE RADIO YEARS 1939-1955 (Meteor)
The single most comprehensive survey of Sinatra's involvement with radio, including two broadcasts with Harry James, 18 with Tommy Dorsey and the rest taken from airshots featuring the solo Sinatra, including 20 from the *To Be Perfectly Frank* series. 125 items in all, compiled by the author who also wrote the in-depth booklet and analysis of the contents of this six-CD boxed set. **37, 118**

SONGS BY SINATRA, VOLUME ONE * (PJ International Records)
Two complete broadcasts from the series from February and November 1946, both co-starring the one-and-only Jimmy Durante as

well as the Pied Pipers. Mostly music, but Sinatra-Durante team up for comedy sketches.

TOMMY DORSEY & HIS ORCHESTRA (Jazz Hour)
Emanating from the Hollywood Palladium in 1940 and including "The One I Love", "Our Love Affair", "Shadows On The Sand" and "That's How It Goes".

TOMMY DORSEY & HIS ORCHESTRA – LIVE AT THE MEADOWBROOK
(Jasmine). Two complete shows – one from the Meadowbrook in 1941 (featuring Sinatra singing "Everything Happens To Me"; "Oh! Look At Me Now"; "Let's Get Away From It All"), and the second from the Capitol, Washington, DC ("Just As I Thought You Were Here"; "You Are Always In My Heart"; "Snootie Little Cutie"). **37**

TOMMY DORSEY & HIS ORCHESTRA: 1942 WAR BOND BROADCAST
(Jazz Hour). Three Sinatra contributions to this particular war-drive broadcast, plus further Sinatra-Dorsey gems ("Blues In The Night"; "Somebody Loves Me"; "Dig Down Deep") from two other shows.

THE UNHEARD FRANK SINATRA, VOLUME ONE: "AS TIME GOES BY" (Vintage Jazz Classics)/**VOLUME TWO: "THE HOUSE I LIVE IN": EARLY ENCORES 1943-1946** (VJC)/**VOLUME THREE: "LONG AGO & FAR AWAY": RADIO RARITIES 1943-1949** (VJC)/**VOLUME FOUR: "I'LL BE SEEING YOU"** (VJC). The most interesting and comprehensive series of Forties material, mostly culled from radio shows and rehearsals of shows. Vols. I & II are taken from recently-discovered 16" radio discs, in pristine condition. Vol. III is perhaps even more significant: along with radio excerpts, it contains Hollywood Bowl concert material (1945, 1948) of superb quality. **74**

YOUNG FRANK SINATRA: IN THE BLUE OF EVENING
(Natasha Imports). 27 tracks featuring a consistently rewarding batch of 1943 War Transcriptions, plus a quartet of Government Transcriptions from 1948, 1952.

Recordings of Gigs

FOR THE GOOD TIMES (Boardwalk)
Extracts from Sinatra gigs at Resorts International, Atlantic City, 1979. 16 individual performances in all.

FRANK SINATRA: A MAN & HIS MUSIC (Golden Age)
Two separate programmes: Consistently fine singing at a concert from November 1965 forms the major part of this CD. The rest comprises short, one-chorus versions of a dozen Sinatra favourites, recorded in Italy during the world tour for a commercial project involving local TV.

FRANK SINATRA LIVE, VOLUME 4 (Golden Age)
Rumoured at one time to have been taped by Capitol for release as Sinatra's first live album, this splendid 18-song performance was recorded in Seattle, Washington, in June 1957. Nelson Riddle conducts as Frank reprises classics such as "You Make Me Feel So Young", "The Lady Is A Tramp"' "My Funny Valentine"' "One For My Baby"... and sings his latest single, "Hey! Jealous Lover", under protest... !

FRANK SINATRA – LIVE IN ITALY (Disc Magic)
A well-produced, triple-pack CD set celebrating three separate visits to Italy. The first finds him accompanied by the Bill Miller Sextet during his 1962 charity world tour; Disc Two has Miller directing the John Flanagan Orchestra, 24 years later; the third has Sinatra with Ultimate Event compadres, Minnelli and Davis, in 1989, and, like the other two, was recorded in Milan. Two bonus tracks, including the "High Hopes" promo disc for JFK ... plus a personal "We Thank You, Frank" vocal tribute by International Sinatra Society President, Gary Doktor ...

FRANK SINATRA & SEXTET LIVE IN PARIS [1962] Reprise

FRANK SINATRA: MONTE CARLO 1958 (JRRecords)
Complete concert, introduced inimitably by Noel Coward, before the Monaco Royal Family, plus other distinguished guests. Customary Sinatra fare – including "I've Got You Under My Skin", "April In Paris", "I Get A Kick Out Of You" and "You Make Me Feel So Young" (a request-encore for Princess Grace), plus an uninhibited "Road To Mandalay". **119-121**

FRANK SINATRA: WASHINGTON, DC, 1973

(JRRecords). Sinatra at the White House – and introduced by "Tricky Dicky" himself – just prior to the re-emergence of Ol' Blue Eyes. Easing his way back into the vocal limelight, with 10 numbers. Not yet back to top form, maybe, but sounding good on the likes of "One For My Baby", "I Have Dreamed", "Try A Little Tenderness" and, of course, patriotic-plus on "The House I Live In"... **140**

SALOON SINGER (Encore Records).

Two-thirds of the never-released Reprise-cut Live-at-the-Sands session in November 1961 (including "Moonlight In Vermont"; "Here's That Rainy Day"; "In The Still Of The Night"; "Please Be Kind"), plus all his solo items (*sans* Martin, Davis) at the Villa Venice, Chicago, gig of December 1962.

SINATRA IN THE SPOTLIGHT * (Retrospect, 2 LPs)

With orchestra conducted by Don Costa, Sinatra sounds inspired by the enthusiastic response from a packed Montreal Auditorium in May 1975. Repertoire includes revived oldies, "But Beautiful", "This Love Of Mine" and "Put Your Dreams Away", the usual regulars, plus the Jenkins-arranged, Legrand-composed "Saddest Thing Of All", recorded the previous fall, but never to be officially released ...

THE SINATRA SAGA (Bravura)

39 live performances, encompassing the Fifties-through-the-Eighties and including excerpts from a 1959 Australian concert with the Red Norvo Quintet and a trio of numbers with the Basie Band in the Sixties. All in all the Voice doesn't sound too bad. **121**

THE SINATRA SAGA, VOLUME 2 (Bravura)

20 more live tracks from 1976 to 1986. The voice tends to sound a tad more roughed-up on the later performances (e.g. "Here's To The Band", "Change Partners"). Overall sound, like its predecessors, is good. **121**

SINATRA: THE PARIS CONCERT/RECORDED LIVE AT THE LIDO, JUNE 5, 1962 (Encore).

The title says it all – one of the world charity tour concerts, with Sinatra in sparkling form throughout this 23-number concert. Bill Miller leads a spirited sextet from the piano. "Moonlight In Vermont", "Night & Day", and, yes, both 'April in Paris' and "I Love Paris" feature among the titles. **137**

VINTAGE SINATRA, VOL. 2 * (Sinatra Society Of Australia)

Fine presentation (including insert card with repertoire information and press reaction to what was a magnificent Sinatra performance). Vibist Red Norvo fronts a solid jazz quintet (augmented by local big band at the end), as Frank freewheels through "I Could Have Danced All Night", "At Long Last Love", "Dancing In The Dark", plus "Willow, Weep For Me", and "Moonlight In Vermont". **121**

The inimitable "Satchmo" – a memorable TV duettist with Sinatra.

TV

THE EDSEL SHOW * (Loota)

The legendary CBS/TV special of 13 October 1957, hosted by Crosby and co-starring Louis Armstrong and Rosemary Clooney. Bob Hope makes a surprise cameo appearance during the World Tour Medley. The Sinatra-Armstrong "Birth Of The Blues" is, in Sinatra parlance, a "gasser". **117**

"SINATRA": MUSIC FROM THE CBS MINI-SERIES

(Warners, 2 CDs). 26 original FS recordings – one with Harry James, six with Tommy Dorsey, plus material from Columbia, Capitol and Reprise (1944-79). Also included are tracks by Crosby (2), Benny Goodman, Billie Holiday. **153**

WE'D LOVE TO HAVE YOU * (Castagna)

A brace of late-Fifties Sinatra TV shows – featuring the McGuire Sisters (15/11/57) and Eddie Fisher (28/3/58) respectively. Great Sinatra singing on both: on the first, "Three Coins In The Fountain", "Baby, Won't You Please Come Home?", on the second: "Taking A Chance On Love", "Time After Time".

WE'VE GOT THE NUMBERS OTHERS DREAM ABOUT! * (Castagna).

Two more Sinatra TV shows – the first with Van Johnson as special guest (28/2/58); the second with Edie Adams and Stan Freberg (7/3/58). Frank scores with "Come Fly With Me", "There's No You"; then, with an electrifying "I'm Gonna Live Till I Die" and a touching "One For My Baby" on the latter show.

Movies

THE SOUNDTRACK SESSIONS (Bravura)

A marvellous collection of Sinatra' movie items. All nine songs from the soundtrack of *Meet Danny Wilson* (including an alternative take of "I've Got A Crush On You"), supported by his exhilarating vocal contributions to the never-completed *Finian's Rainbow* animation project (including duets with Ella and Louis Armstrong). If all that isn't enough, there are the vocals from *The Joker Is Wild*, plus "If I Loved You" (from *Carousel*, the movie from which Frank walked), the unreleased title tune from *The Man With The Golden Arm* and the song Sinatra recorded specially for *Advise & Consent*.   108

Videography

Movies

TV:

Filmography

Step Lively – but that's the last thing on Frank's mind.

Index

Picture Credits

The publishers would like to thank the following sources for their kind permission to reproduce the photographs in this book:

Hulton Deutsch Collection 56, 120/1, 137, 138; **London Features International** 4(top right), 4(top centre right), 4(bottom centre right), 9, 11, 16, 25, 30, 33, 38, 39, 40, 42, 46, 57, 60, 61, 65, 67, 70, 81, 85, 87, 88, 90, 96, 103, 106, 108, 112, 116, 117, 127, 132(bottom left), 136, 141(bottom), 141, 147, 151, 157; **Pictorial Press** 4(bottom centre), 10, 26, 27, 28/9, 35, 52, 53, 54, 55, 62, 66, 68, 69, 71, 72, 73, 76, 82, 89, 92/3, 95, 99, 100, 101, 104, 107, 109, 113, 115, 122/3, 125, 126, 131, 135, 136, 155; **Range Bettmann UPI** 4(bottom right), 4(top centre), 4(centre middle top), 4(bottom left), 4(bottom centre left), 4(top centre left), 4(centre middle bottom), 6/7, 13, 14/5, 16, 19, 20, 22, 36, 41, 43, 44, 45, 48, 49, 50, 51, 58, 63, 64, 69, 75, 78/9, 79, 80, 84, 97, 98, 110, 111, 119, 128, 132/3, 138, 139, 140, 142, 143, 159; **Rex Features** 153, Dezo Hoffmann 132, 156, Nils Jorgensen 145, LGI 148/9, Yoram Kahana 150, SIPA 18, 21, Richard Young 3.